Bookbinding with Adhesives

Second Edition

Bookbinding with Adhesives

Second Edition

Tony Clark FIOP

McGRAW-HILL BOOK COMPANY

London · New York · St Louis · San Francisco · Auckland
Bogotá · Caracas · Lisbon · Madrid · Mexico · Milan
Montreal · New Delhi · Panama · Paris · San Juan
São Paulo · Singapore · Sydney · Tokyo · Toronto

Published by
McGRAW-HILL Book Company Europe
Shoppenhangers Road, Maidenhead, Berkshire, SL6 2QL, England
Telephone 0628 23432
Fax 0628 770224

British Library Cataloguing in Publication Data

Clark, Tony
Bookbinding with Adhesives. – 2Rev.ed
I. Title
686.35
ISBN 0-07-707985-X

Library of Congress Cataloging-in-Publication Data

Clark, Tony.
Bookbinding with adhesives / Tony Clark. - 2nd ed.
p. cm.
ISBN 0-07-707985-X
1. Bookbinding. 2. Adhesives. I. Title.
Z271.3.A34C57 1994
686.3-dc20 93-45647
CIP

12345 HBL 97654

Typeset by BookEns Ltd, Baldock, Herts.
This book block is unsewn bound (perfect bound) bonded with the second generation reactive hotmelt (Purfect 563). It has been applied via a Nordson unit.
Printed and bound in Great Britain by BPC Hazell Books Ltd

This book is dedicated to all my friends in the bookbinding industry worldwide.

My thanks to Marion for her support during the conception and my note-making at odd hours.

Contents

List of diagrams

Note on measurements

1 kp (kilopond) = 1 kg = 10 N = 2.2 lb

1 in = 25 mm

0.5 mm = 20 thou or 0.02 in

1 lb/in = 1 lb/2.5 cm

= 0.4 lb/cm

$$\therefore \frac{0.4}{2.2} = 0.18 \text{ kp/cm} = 1.8 \text{ N/cm}$$

Preface

The purpose of this book is to provide a guide for managers and machine operators on machine settings, substrates to be bonded and other data for the bindery.

It should also make profitable reading for students of printing and book production. It is not intended as an adhesive chemist's handbook.

The book covers adhesive types and how they work, and the various systems of using them: unsewn, one-shot, multi-coat, burst and case binding.

Every problem cannot be solved in this one book, nor can every system and machine be covered in full, but it should give a good background knowledge of adhesives to newcomers to the industry as well as enhancing or refreshing the knowledge of the more experienced.

The future

Adhesive technology advances inconceivably slowly most of the time, but with sudden bursts of new technical achievement. One thing is certain: development will not stop.

So when this book has gone to bed and within a short while, new methods will be talked about, but they will not be seen in the general trade until they have been proven safe to use, or machines have been adapted, or built to use them.

Third generation reactive hotmelts (PUR) with faster bond times yet increased pot life and biodegradable or 100% dispersible spine adhesives will be the goal for the development chemists. New 'Twinflex' two-shot (emulsion/hotmelt) with an aqueous hardener and a special hotmelt is just around the corner. I look forward to the future.

Tony Clark

1 Types of adhesive and how they work

Animal glues

These are mainly used for case making and lining, and only occasionally in unsewn binding lines. Animal glues consist of one or more kinds of gelatine in a solution of water. They give aggressive tack with a medium-set speed. Such glues are available in slab jelly form, or as harder granules. Since animal glues are derived from natural materials, they are much subject to seasonal factors and tend to vary with their source of supply. Operators using them have to be skilled in achieving the right degree of dilution and tack. Most animal glues age and become brittle under dry, warm conditions, as is normally evident from the condition of the spine of a book kept for some time in a centrally heated home.

Starches and dextrines

Starches derived from maize, potato and tapioca are used for producing pastes, generally for the hand-binding section of the trade. However, some are used in operations such as endpapering and tipping, also hand case making in leather. Starches can be modified into dextrines, which increases their solid content and their tack and speed. Although dextrines are not used widely in the binding industry, they still find favour in some tipping and labelling applications.

Emulsions

An emulsion adhesive is a dispersion, in a water 'carrier', of solid particles, together with additives, to produce bonding properties that have been tailor-made for their applications. PVA, EVA and other adhesives each have a synthetic basis, but may have many other products, synthetic or natural, added to make up a particular end-formula. Emulsion adhesives can vary in pH, i.e. acidity or alkalinity, in solid content, and in physical characteristics, for example low-viscosity high-solids, high-viscosity low-solids, very fast setting or quite slow, brittle or flexible.

In bookbinding, emulsion adhesives are used on endpapers, for tipping, for gluing-off operations, for lining, casing-in, spine gluing and side gluing, and on special stencil applicator case makers. They are widely used in unsewn binding as primers for special hotmelts and in other one-shot and multi-shot applications. Some can be reactivated, others are easily dried by radio-frequency units. All emulsion adhesives dry by the loss of the water carrier.

Hotmelts

Hotmelts adhesives are 100 per cent solid thermoplastic materials that flow when heated; the final bond is gained when the temperature has fallen to the ambient one, i.e. that of the material being glued. Hotmelts consist of polymers, tackifying resins, and waxes; they have the distinct advantages of being capable of extremely high tack with medium to very fast setting speeds, and of not necessitating nightly cleaning down of equipment.

Hotmelts are used mainly as one-shot adhesives for pocket-books and magazines, in multi-shot applications in the production of catalogues, and in burst binding, which, combined with a stretch lining material, may be used when a book is to be rounded and backed.

Modern hotmelts can bond the widest possible range of paper stocks, and if formulated correctly have yet to reveal any age limit.

(PUR) or reactive hotmelts

These products are 100 per cent solid moisture curing hotmelts. They are produced from a range of polymers which are blended in a special reactor. In the presence of moisture they crosslink and form a tough skin that resists re-melting; this also gives them a high degree of heat, cold and solvent resistance far beyond normal hotmelts. The second generation reactive hotmelts have high tack levels thus reducing the need for special laydown or conveying systems and they can also be trimmed or sawn within a minute.

Reactive hotmelts are mainly used for unsewn binding on difficult papers that would normally have been sewn, to give and hold a good round on a sewn or unsewn book block. Laboratory tests have not yet found an age limit on these products.

Principles of adhesion

The mechanism of adhesion

Even a surface that is 'optically flat' will in fact appear very rough when it is examined under high enough magnification, i.e. on a molecular scale. Therefore, no two surfaces can ever be in 100 per cent contact, and in fact any two surfaces will seldom be in contact over more than 10 per cent of their common area. They can be bonded together in two basic ways, as follows:

Mechanical adhesion This works only with absorbent materials: the polymer molecules in the adhesive between the surfaces interlock with them by penetrating the crevices of each of the two surfaces to be bonded. In a similar way, a haystack is held together purely by the mechanical forces involved in the intermingling of the grass stems. Mechanical adhesion is the prime contributing factor to bond strength in gluing paper to paper and rubber to textiles.

Chemical or specific adhesion Chemical adhesion is due to primary bonds resulting from specific primary valency bonds.

This is the main theory of adhesion and involves secondary Van der Waals surface forces, these forces being responsible for the molecular attractions, i.e. cohesive forces in plastic materials, liquids, etc. Such forces only act over very short distances and therefore for two substances to be stuck together by them they must be brought into very intimate contact; hence the importance for good 'wetting out' of the adherends by the adhesive. The best adhesives are therefore mobile liquids, that readily wet out the substrates. By the same reasoning, a flexible natural rubber would be a better adhesive than the less flexible SBR rubbers or the still less flexible styrene polymers.

Adhesives and recyclability

Adhesives classed as recyclable

1 An adhesive that comes away from the fibres, leaving no contaminates in the water or the finished product.

2 The adhesive is fully incorporated into the finished product and becomes an integral part of the fibres of that product.

Adhesives classed as non-recyclable

1 Products that contaminate the water system or mechanical mechanism of the paper making machine.

2 Animal glues once classed as recyclable are now regarded as undesirable due to their high biological oxygen demand (BOD) as they are basically a protein.

Chemical and other terms

Adhesive, cohesive, adherend Cohesive forces are the forces responsible for substances such as polythene, rubber, etc., having rigid shapes, i.e. the forces acting between the molecules within a substance, whereas adhesive forces are similar forces acting between the molecules of dissimilar substances, e.g. between paint and metal. An adhesive is the substance used to bond together two adherends (substrates).

Blocking An undesirable adhesion between touching layers of a material such as occurs under moderate pressure during storage.

Coating weight The amount of adhesive expressed as

weight per unit area (e.g. grams per square metre) required to give the most satisfactory bond. It is sometimes expressed as film thickness (in thousandths of millimetres), either wet or dry.

Consistency The property of an adhesive (paste) that causes it to resist deformation. (*See* note under 'Viscosity'.)

Cooling time The time required to allow a hot fluid adhesive to become firm and trimmable.

Creep Creep results when a shear force is applied to substrates bonded with an adhesive of relatively low cohesive strength, e.g. when hanging a weight on a lap joint.

Cure A chemical reaction (cross-linking) which results in a physical change (hardening or setting). It is brought about by means of increasing the temperature, contact with moisture or adding a catalyst and the change is irreversible.

Drying speed The time needed to form a final bond. This may or may not be the same as the setting speed.

Heat seal A heat-seal adhesive is one in which the dried film is activated by heating immediately before bond formation.

Heat set A heat-set adhesive is one that forms its bonds on the application of heat and in which the water present is absorbed internally to form a gel. National Starch and Chemical Corporation has patented this process.

Open time The time between applying adhesive to one or both of the substrates and bringing them together.

Paste Starch-and-water or other adhesive with the consistency of thick cream, i.e. non-pourable.

Peel The force used to measure the adhesive strength of a pressure-sensitive adhesive. This is usually 180° peel, i.e. the substrate or is pulled (peeled) back on itself.

Penetration The entry of the adhesive into the substrate(s). It invariably occurs to a greater extent with the substrate on to which the adhesive is coated.

Plasticizer A material added to an adhesive in order to render the dry film of adhesive more flexible. An *external* plasticizer is incorporated in the adhesive as an addition after polymerization is complete, whereas an *internal* plasticizer is added during the polymerization process and forms an integral part of the polymer used as the adhesive base.

Pressure sensitive An adhesive is pressure-sensitive that adheres to a surface at room temperature when only pressure is briefly applied. Such adhesives are permanently tacky.

PUR polyurethane/reactive hotmelt First generation PURs were 100 per cent polyurethane, but generation improvements in performance have been gained with the addition of other ingredients, so reactive hotmelts still cross-link due to the polyurethane constitutent. Hence the title PUR/reactive hotmelt.

Radio-frequency or high frequency A technique for bonding two substances together in which the glue line is heated by means of radio-frequency electromagnetic waves. This process is particularly suitable for substrates that would be damaged by the application of direct heat, since the substrate itself is not heated.

Rheology The study of the deformation and flow of matter, and hence of a multitude of physical properties. Adhesives with the same viscosity but different rheological properties will behave differently on the same machine.

Setting speed The time taken to form a handling bond (or initial bond) under heat, pressure, etc., by means of a chemical or physical change.

Shortness Lack of stringing, cobwebbing, or formation of threads during application, e.g. during the separation of a stereo and a roller.

Solids content That part of an adhesive left after all solvent has been driven off by heating. It is always expressed as a percentage.

Tack The ability of an adhesive to form an initial bond of measurable strength immediately after the adhesive and adherend are brought into intimate contact by only very light pressure.

Thermoplastic, thermosetting A thermoplastic material is one that will soften on heating and return to its original state on cooling, the process being indefinitely repeatable. A thermosetting material is one that undergoes a chemical change on heating, giving a solid material that does not revert to its original state on cooling; the change is irreversible.

Thixotropy, dilatency A thixotropic system is one that thins out when stirred but reverts to its original consistency on standing. A dilatent system has the opposite properties, i.e. it thickens on agitation.

Viscosity The aggregate of the forces within a liquid (adhesive) that tend to prevent the liquid from flowing. **Note** Viscosity and consistency are not synonymous.

Wetting The ability of an adhesive to 'flow out' (wet) a surface by coming into intimate (molecular) contact with it.

Principles of hotmelts and emulsions

Having discussed the different methods by which adhesives form the final bond, let us consider briefly how hotmelts and emulsions work.

In the case of an emulsion, which is a stabilized suspension of discrete particles in water, the stabilization forces are fairly weak, so that when the solids content reaches about 65-70 per cent these forces are overcome and the emulsion particles coalesce to give a continuous film with strength. Thus an emulsion will give initial fibre tear while 20-25 per cent of the water still remains in the film. Thus a PVA *emulsion* bonds about twice as fast as a dextrine *solution* of the same viscosity and solids content.

A hotmelt forms its bond by cooling. Since a *little* hotmelt is placed on a large surface to be bonded at room temperature, it cools rapidly and hence gives fibre tear in 1-5 seconds.

Thus hotmelts are the quickest to form bonds (by cooling), emulsions the next quickest (by coalescence of the suspension) and solutions slowest (by penetration and loss of carrier).

Choice of hotmelt and its supplier

Which hotmelt do you choose? It *must* be manufactured

and sold by the same company. They must give you proof of quality controls and must show batch-marking systems clearly on their containers. Before you put a hotmelt anywhere near your binder the following questions must be asked and the answers conveyed to your adhesive supplier:

1 What are your major paper stocks?

2 Does the book have to meet hot or very cold conditions?

3 Will the ink used in the printing have traces of solvent (white spirit), etc. left in it?

4 Will the machine be used every day?

5 What are the highest and slowest speeds you wish to run at?

6 What is the method of spine preparation?

7 What is the time from the binder to the trimmer at its high speed?

8 Do you require the company to supply one-shot, or two-shot?

How to choose the right type of adhesive: 'MS/ECP'

The letters 'MS/ECP' are the key to a convenient checklist for discovering which specific adhesive you require. These letters stand for the five basic factors that you have to consider:

M - Make of machine and model number.
Method of adhesive application.
Measurement in time from application to compression.
Measurement in time from compression to next operation, etc.

S - Substrates to be bonded together.
Subsequent operations.
Systems other than adhesives being used after the gluing operation.

E - End use of final product, e.g. export.
Exposure to cold or hot conditions.

Environmental standards to be met.

C - Cost effectiveness.
Current products used.
Colour and odour importance.
Conditions of storage.
Container and consignment sizes.

P - Plant conditions: humidity, temperature, housekeeping.
Personnel requirements: easy cleaning, low odour, non-staining, etc.

If when you order an adhesive you use this list to detail your requirements, and provide substrate samples, it is likely that your supplier will submit an adhesive that will perform on your machinery and meet the standards to which you will subject the bonded article.

MS/ECP is a National Starch and Chemical Corporation concept developed for worldwide use.

2 Testing for paper grain

The paper you intend to bind contains a grain, which is created by the flow of the pulp stock as it is suspended on the endless wire belt of the paper machine (Figure 2.1).

Figure 2.1
Grain direction

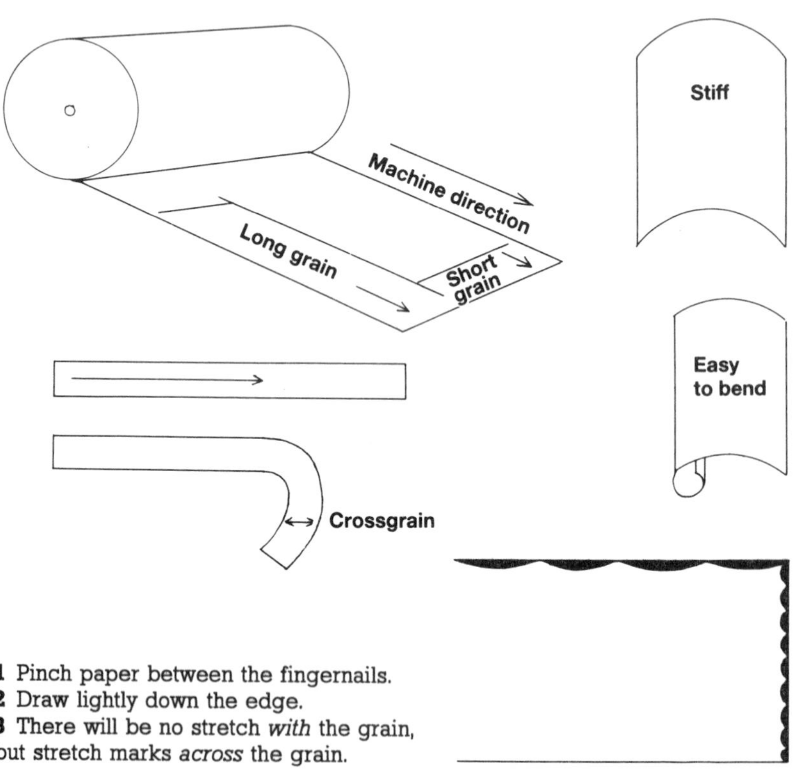

1 Pinch paper between the fingernails.
2 Draw lightly down the edge.
3 There will be no stretch *with* the grain, but stretch marks *across* the grain.

Figure 2.1 (*cont.*)

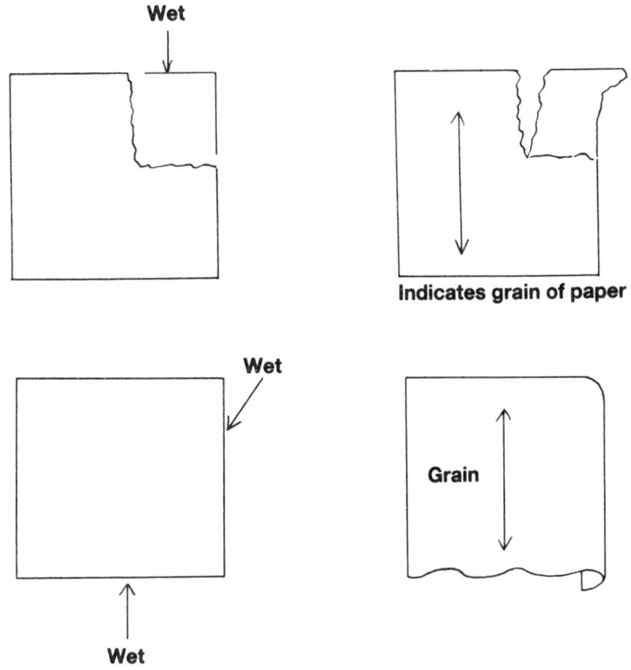

Wet

Indicates grain of paper

Wet

Grain

Wet

Long grain

This is cut lengthwise from the paper web, so that the direction of travel parallels the longer side.

Short grain

This is cut crosswise from the paper web, so that the grain runs across the shorter side.

3 Preparation of signatures

Inspection of signatures

Inspect the signatures to see that they have been folded correctly. If they are badly folded, have a look at the perforations. Sections should be smashed to avoid having a hole in the centre of the signature that will allow hotmelt to penetrate between the centre pages as soon as the fold or bolt has been cut off. Also, if most of the signatures are folded well, but one of them badly, or badly damaged in transportation, then hotmelt will penetrate between the good and the badly folded signatures again after the folds have been cut off (Figure 3.1).

Figure 3.1
Inspection of signatures

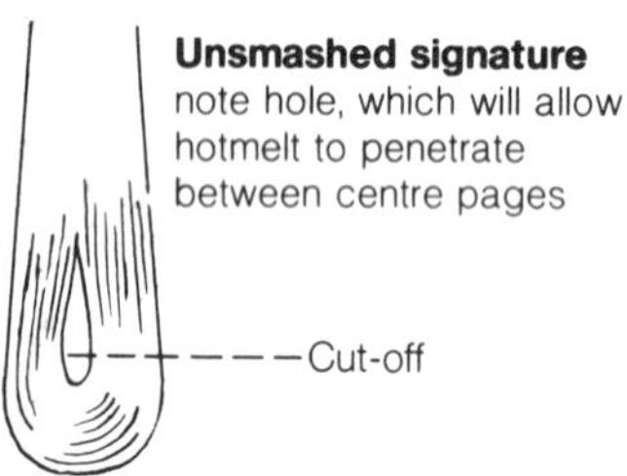

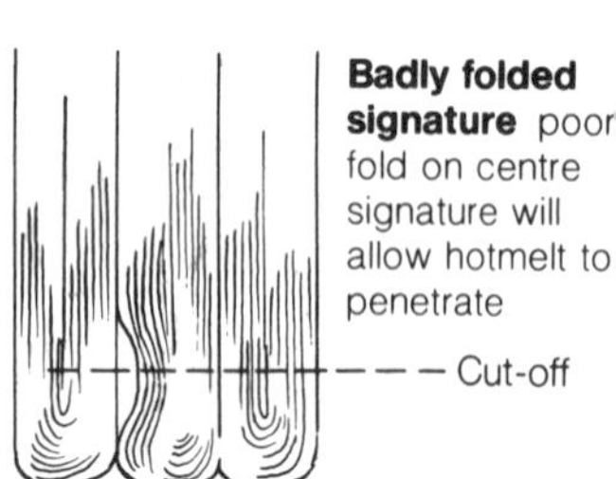

Cut-off depth

The next operation is to remove the folds or bolts. The depth of cut depends on the amount of pages in signature Figure 3.2), the bulk of the paper and the amount of gully that has been allowed, also the tightness of the spine fold. The normal allowance when pages are laid down is 3 mm for the cut-off.

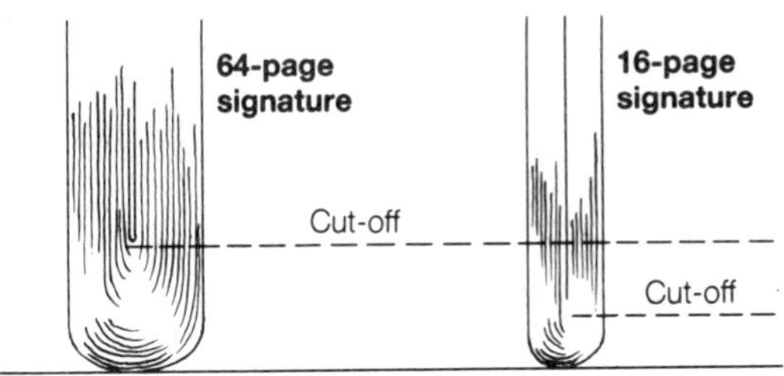

Figure 3.2
Depth of cut

Cutting knives and cutting saws

The cutting off is done by a knife or knives of some form, a saw, or a combined miller/rougher (Figures 3.3 and 3.4).

3

Spine-cutting units

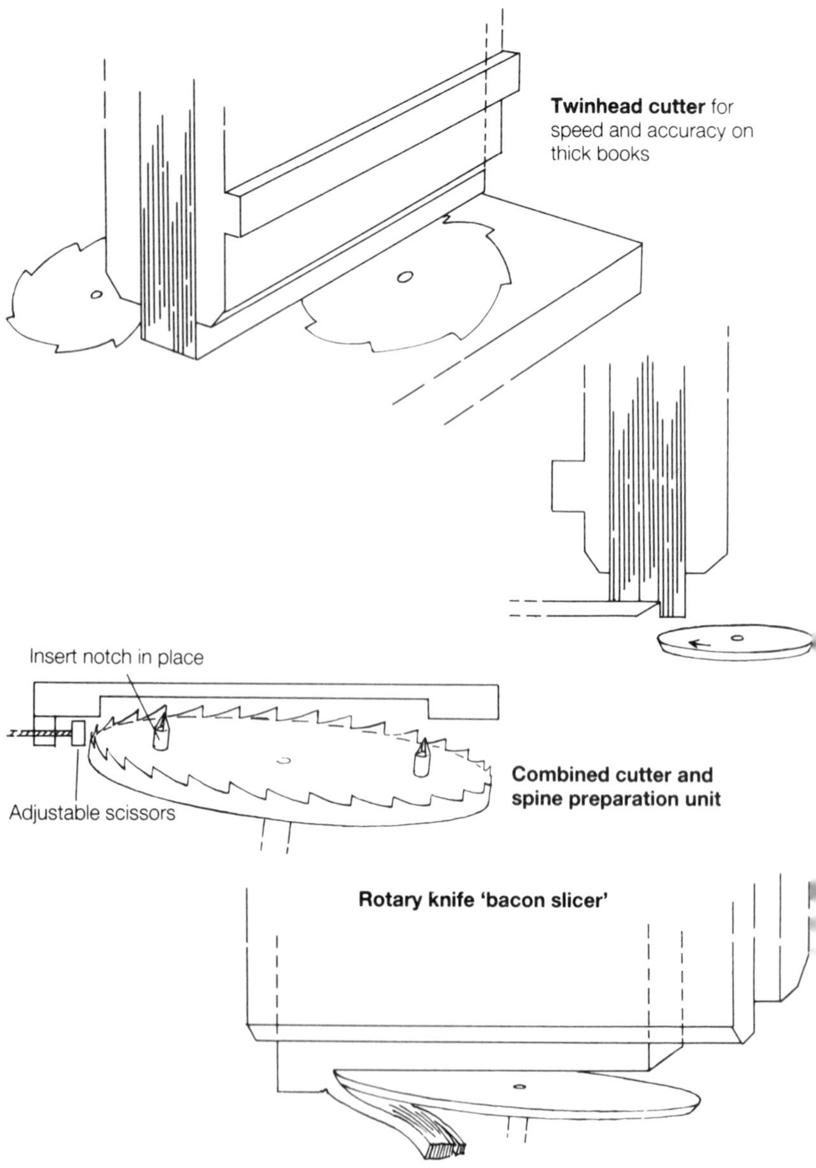

Figure 3.3 Spine-cutting units

Cutter backup units

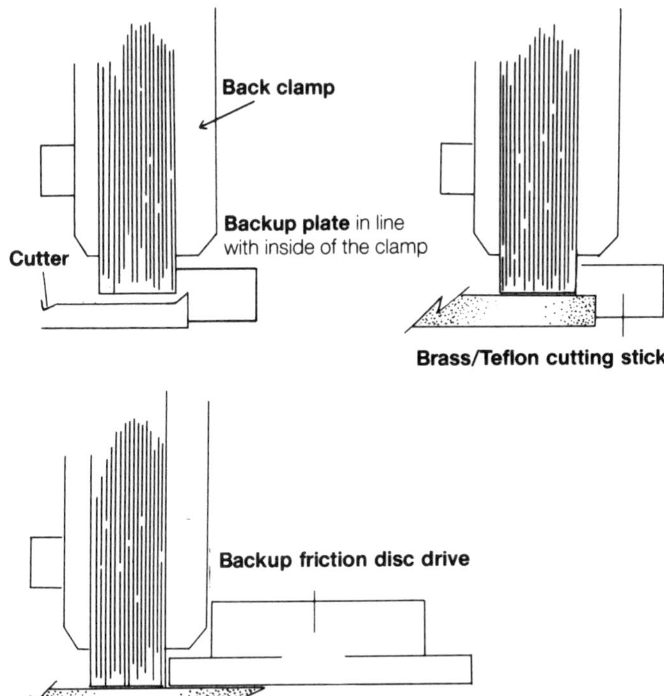

Figure 3.4
Cutter backup units

The preparation of the spine is one of the most important operations in adhesive binding. The finish must be the same from the front of the book block to the back and must not vary from head to tail. If there is any variation then there must be a mechanical misalignment or undue wear and tear.

Milling knives

These normally cut off the folds on the smaller binding machines. The scrap is not saleable as it is reduced to dust. It is important to keep the knives very sharp, especially on machines that do not have a backup plate.

Shredding head

This cuts the bolts off cleanly in shreds. These can be compressed, bundled and sold for repulping. The spine is so smooth that after this operation a separate preparation unit has to be used. The heads are set at an angle so that they cut with the leading edge only and just miss the book block with the training edge. This helps to reduce down-drag and heat.

Rotary knife ('bacon slicer')

Units of this type can normally be sharpened on the run. They slice off the bolts cleanly, producing a very smooth spine which again must be prepared before a one-shot hotmelt is used. The knife is normally tilted slightly to reduce drag and minimize the heat. However, if the knife is set at too sharp an angle a concave cut will result. During the cutting operation the paper must be supported by a backstop and the aligning of this stop or of friction drive discs is extremely important. Some machines have a backup plate and scissor bar.

Machines fitted with discs

The bottom of the book protruding from the clamp is supported by two discs (Figure 3.5), as follows:

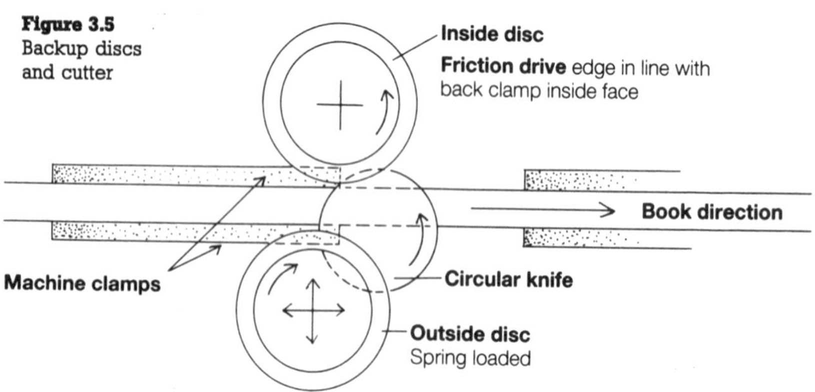

Figure 3.5
Backup discs and cutter

Inside disc

This is set so that it is driven by friction by the rotary knife, or on some machines by the movement of the clamp. The disc should revolve when there is no book in the clamp. Only finger pressure should be required to stop it; if it takes more than this, the pressure on the cutter is too tight.

Outside disc

This is spring-loaded with an adjustment for different thicknesses of books; it also has left, right, forward, and backward adjustments.

Note Some binding machines have much larger discs than the circular knife. These can be friction-driven from the clamp as well as by contact with the book; in this case the gap between the circular knife and the base of the inside disc must not be greater than half the thickness of the paper being bound.

Roughening units

For these units to work successfully they must be extremely sharp, cut cleanly and have a good system of evacuating the chad or scrap they create. It is no good cutting a notch if it is filled with loose clay or fibres, since hotmelt will then stick only to this loose material. Several types of roughening units exist (Figure 3.6 overleaf), as follows:

Bandsaw

This unit normally has carbon-tipped teeth, which produce a fluffy feel and are ideal for very fibrous papers and when the emulsion-hotmelt Twinflex systems are being used.

Rotary head

This has notching units attached to the side. When the notch becomes blunt, the disc can be rotated so that a new surface is available to cut the notch. The head is offset by some 15°, so that it mills only as it enters the front of the book block and emerges from the back. The

Figure 3.6 Roughening units: saw, notch and sanding disc types

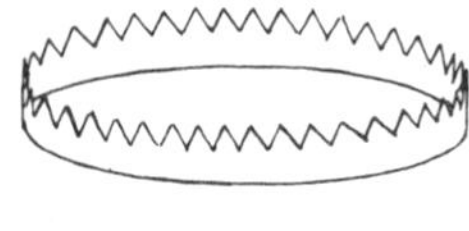

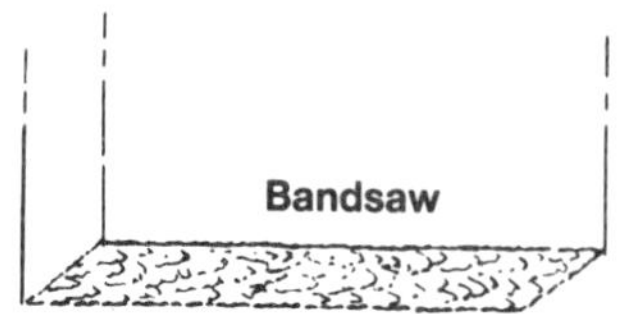

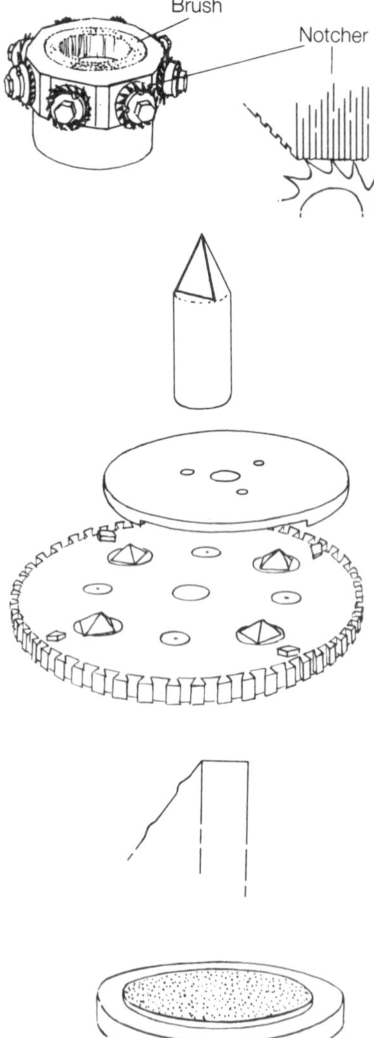

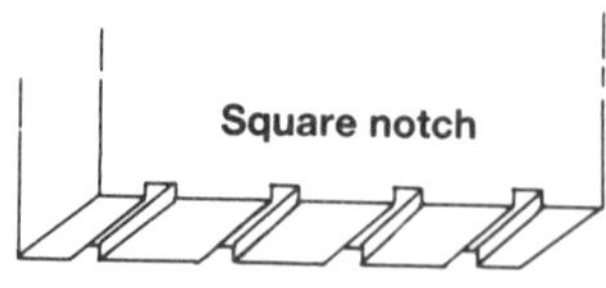

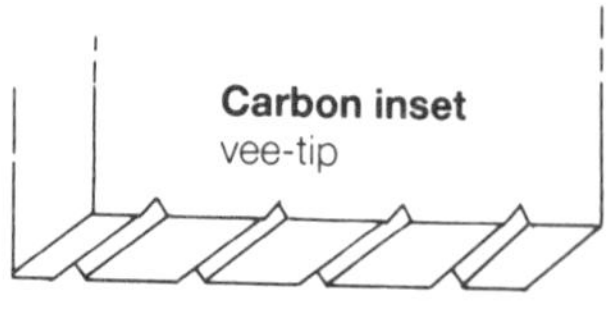

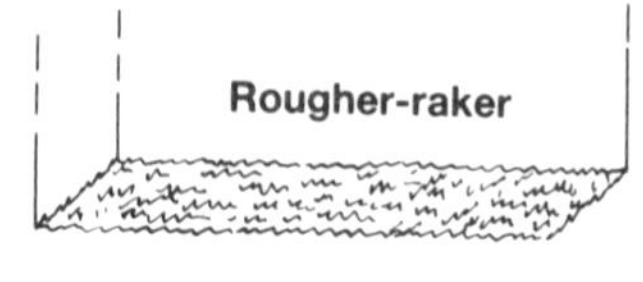

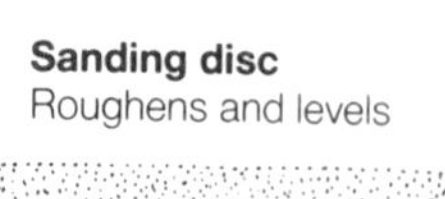

notches look as though they have been cut by a square blade.

Carbon bit

This is generally a round, sharpened tool which produces a vee-shaped notch. Vee-shaped notches normally expose fibres, even when there are papers of different grains in one book block. If backing discs are available, care should be taken to see that they are kept in good condition and aligned, since they act as a cutting stick and if not used correctly will give a ragged inside edge that will spoil the look of the book by imparting a one-sided 'nail-head' appearance on the inside of the book block. Some cutting spindles can be set up so that only the leading edge of the roughening unit comes into contact with the paper.

Rougher–raker

This is a specialized unit. After the notches are cut, a carbon block attached to the unit rips out the chips, thus forming a fibrous anchor for hotmelt. Some roughening units have centre sections with interchangeable plates, such as sanding discs, wire teasers and rotary brushes.

Sanding disc

This is used to increase fibre and imparts a fluffy texture to the spine, when using emulsion or reactive hotmelt adhesives. It can be used on difficult paper stocks, combined with the normal notching unit. Sanding discs also act as levellers especially when they are contra-rotating.

Spine brushes

For cleaning the spine, rotary brushes are obviously the best, especially if they are accompanied by good extraction. Stationary brushes will suffice, providing they are changed regularly, and good extraction should also be available. If wear is observed on the brushes then they must be changed or turned round immediately. Brushes should be flexible, yet firm. If over-stiff bristles are used then paper chippings can be brushed between signatures. Brushes will help to prevent the scrap and chips of paper entering the side-gluing or spine-gluing units. If paper is observed falling into the hotmelt tank then the spine of the book block has not been cleaned sufficiently. It may be worth getting your engineer to produce another stationary brushing unit if you have any doubts at all.

Rotary brushes

Brushes attached to the sanding discs or notching units are necessary, but an independent brush driven against the direction of the book block has been shown by tests to give a cleaner spine; it also cleans out the slots in burst or slotted binding.

4 One-shot hotmelt and PUR-binding

This chapter deals with machine adjustments, adhesive criteria and recommendations. It is without doubt the largest chapter, and the cornerstone of the book. Before you put hotmelt anywhere near the binder, be sure you have read and understood what follows.

Choice of adhesive

The choice of adhesives is yours, but lay down the criteria you want to perform to (*see* p. 8). It may be useful, before reading further, to look back at the terms 'cooling time' and 'open time' as defined in Chapter 1.

The one-shot hotmelt adhesive should have an open time that will tolerate the slowest and the highest speeds of the bookbinding machine, even in the depths of winter. It should have an aggressive and high tack so as to hold on to the heaviest of cover stocks and resist any cover slip.

Trim time should be calculated on the basis of the fastest speed at which the machine can produce a clean, non-smearing trim. This is essential when producing book blocks that may subsequently be coloured or gilded.

Firm hotmelt, open-flat or cold roundable?

A firm, harder, product is generally used for magazines that have inserts, for catalogues and for telephone directories.

Pocket-books, textbooks and bibles require an open-flat hotmelt.

Cold roundables have been developed for some time now and their application proven. They used to have the drawback of very poor trimming or requiring extended cooling periods, but now products can be trimmed within 40 seconds and show many advantages over emulsion binding, including round-retention.

Hotmelt tank and pre-melt tank temperature settings

Hotmelts that are over-cooked will degrade, so pre-melt tanks should always be 10–15 °C below the running temperature of the hotmelt. The application tank should be set at the correct running temperature 30 minutes before the run begins and turned down by 10–15 °C after the run has ended, unless the binder has to be used within the next 30 minutes.

Good-quality pre-melt tanks have fail-safe thermostats fitted, and it is worth having a unit that will electrically isolate the tank if the temperature rises above 210 °C.

Setting the glue rollers

Application rollers should be set correctly (before the run starts). For this, the gaps must be measured between a book block and rollers free of adhesive (Figure 4.1). The reverse spinner must be clean and hot. The spinner scraper must be set so that it leaves no burnt hotmelt on the surface, and the temperature set and checked at 10–20 °C above the running temperature of the hotmelt being used.

Remember that hotmelts work by flowing around exposed fibres. Thus the art of getting a good, one-shot-bound book is to make sure that the temperature of the hotmelt is right, so that you are putting both heat and the right amount of adhesive on to the spine of the book. Before the book block moves on to the cover station, inspect it to see that there is a good coating of hotmelt, that it looks even and bubble-free, and that the book block is square. If the book block looks as though it has been cut at an angle then inspect the backup plates of the cutter and roughening unit. Remember also that it is not possible to square up a badly cut spine on your cover station; you will only distort the book or produce one with good page pull at the front and extremely poor page pull at the back.

All gaps are measured on dry application wheels.

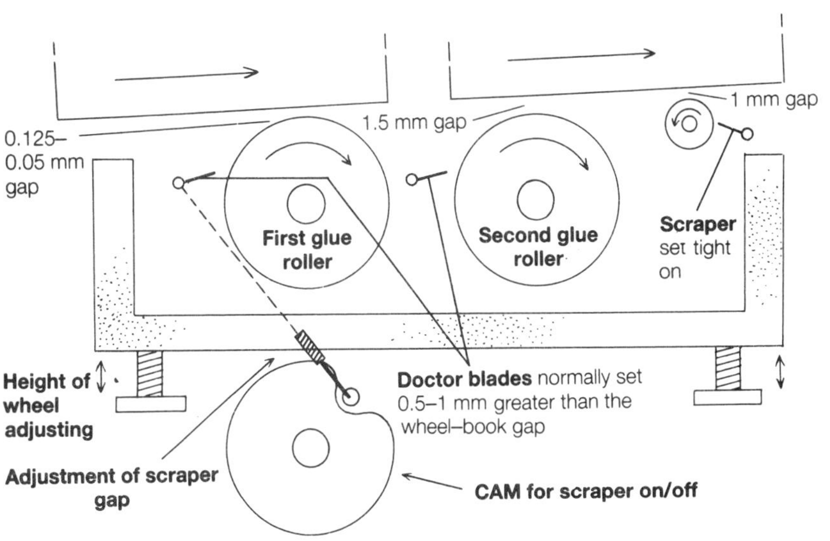

Figure 4.1
Hotmelt tank settings

Adjustment of the first wheel/roller

Set too tight The adhesive will penetrate between the signatures, or the backbone will become a mushroom shape.

Set too lose The adhesive will not wet out the peaks of the notches.

Adjustment of the second wheel

Setting too low The application will be irregular, flooding as the scraper opens and gradually being starved as the adhesive fails to be picked up sufficiently by the application wheel.

Setting too high This will prevent sufficient adhesive being applied.

Adjustment of the reverse spinner Slight adjustments to the reverse spinner may have to be made if it is cooler than it should be, or impossible to keep clean. A cold or dirty spinner will drag more hotmelt off the back of a book than will a clean, hot unit. A dirty spinner is normally due to poor-quality hotmelt, a worn out or badly adjusted scraper, or overheating.

Reverse spinner temperature setting

Most machines are fitted with reverse spinners. Note that the correct temperature is some 10-20 °C above the hotmelt running temperature. Some units do not have temperature controls on their spinners but a simple 1 to 9 number setting for the rheostat. If the scraper is set correctly and the spinner is clean then the temperature at setting 8 is approximately 190 °C, while at setting 9 it is about 200 °C. However, it is important that you get your spinner temperature checked by a non-contact infrared thermometer or a unit with a roll surface probe attachment.

Caution Dirty or misaligned spinners will inevitably produce bad books; make sure that the spinner is clean, hot and level.

Camming facility

This makes it possible to start the spine glue application some 5-10 mm from the head and finish some 5-10 mm from the tail. Caution on setting up is required, so that the trimmed book looks attractive in the spine glue area. The saving of hotmelt can be quite extensive, but the main advantage in camming is the lack of squeeze-out at the cover-drum nip station, which reduces machine downtime for cleaning and also prevents damage to subsequent covers from hotmelt.

Side gluing

Some unsewn-binding machines do not have the ability to apply a side adhesive, and generally, to overcome this, operators will fit wire to form a rib or wall of adhesive that flows up the side of the book block as it passes over the application rollers.

Emulsion side gluing

There are generally three systems of application, as follows:

Ball point nozzle unit

This is gravity-fed and requires a medium-viscosity emulsion that is easy to clean out of the polythene tubing. (Generally, it is better to have a slow-setting emulsion so that the bond is formed when the books are being stacked after three-knife trimming.)

Wheel or disc application

This normally takes place at a position before the hotmelt application. Lines of emulsion are applied by a wheel or disc applicator, which in turn is fed from a roller submerged in emulsion adhesives. Some disc applicators are fed by adhesive climbing up the applicator and being controlled by a simple scraper unit. The correct emulsion should be an easy clean product that is relatively slow, so that it does not skin owing to the movement of heat from the neighbouring hotmelt unit. The bond is formed after the book has been stacked or three-knife trimmed. It is advisable to set the scraper or application wheels so that excess emulsion cannot splash into the hotmelt tank and contaminate the hotmelt. Care should be taken to see that an equal amount of side glue is put on the back and front of the book block.

Extrusion

In this method, a thin bead of emulsion is applied via a nozzle fed from a pressurized storage tank. Several sophisticated on/off devices are available that will facilitate any skip gap or allowances at the head and tail. The adhesive must be pump- and shear-stable, well filtered, and delivered in non-metallic containers.

Hotmelt side gluing

Applicators

The application of hotmelt side gluing can be via a disc

picking up from a hotmelt reservoir, or via a jetting operation controlled by a sophisticated hotmelt unit capable of starting the application a fraction of a millimetre from the head and finishing a fraction of a millimetre from the tail, at whatever speed the binder is being operated.

A function of side glue is to hold the cover so that a hinge can be formed. Also, it makes a magazine or pocket-book look more attractive. Because the speed of binding machines may vary from inching during adjustment to running at extremely high speeds, the time elapsing between the application of the side glue and the arrival of the book at the side-nip unit is going to vary a good deal. The correct type of hotmelt to use is an extended open-time one. The adhesive should bond after the book has left the transporting pocket and is being shingled or carried to the three-knife trimming operation. On most binding machines, the advantage of using a hotmelt with a long open time is that the cover is held away from the book block owing to the design of the machine's clamping systems.

Side gluing hotmelts with precise open times do cause problems. Binding-machine speed varies, as do cover stocks. If the side-nipping unit has not formed the bond immediately then there is no other section on a binder that will assist in its compression. Hotmelt side glues can be applied to the book block or to the cover, provided that the cover has a constant movement as it passes the gluing head.

Cover drum

The cover drum (Figure 4.2) is adjustable vertically and covers should be rolled on. Too much pressure will press out the hotmelt and can cause cover slip, as can too little pressure. The scraper should be controlled to remove any dirt or hotmelt from the drum. With some adhesives, a silicone emulsion needs to be applied via a felt pad to reduce any sticking problems, or there will be transfer of adhesive on to the surface of the next cover.

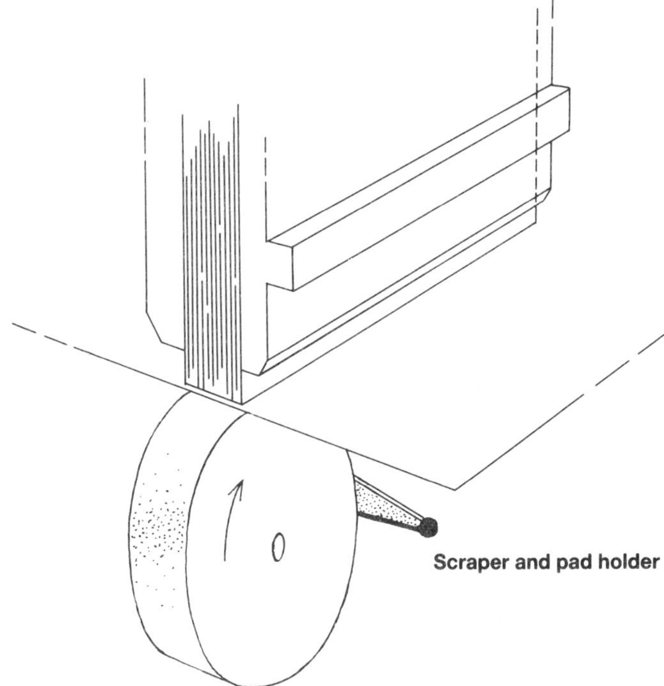

Figure 4.2
Cover drum setting

Cover breaker

The procedure for checking the height of the cover breaker, in other words the gap between the book block and the top dead centre of the backplate, is as follows. Bring the book block in line with no adhesive on it, place a 3 cm wide strip of cover board and cartridge paper at each end of the book, and inch up the cover breaker to its highest point, i.e. the top of the throw (Figure 4.3). Pull out the strips and note the drag. Both strips should feel the same; if they don't then call an engineer to make the necessary adjustment.

Figure 4.4 shows the perfectly adjusted unit. On some machines the backplate cannot be adjusted, so the cut-off, roughening, gluing, and cover drum sections have to be adjusted to accommodate the gap between the book

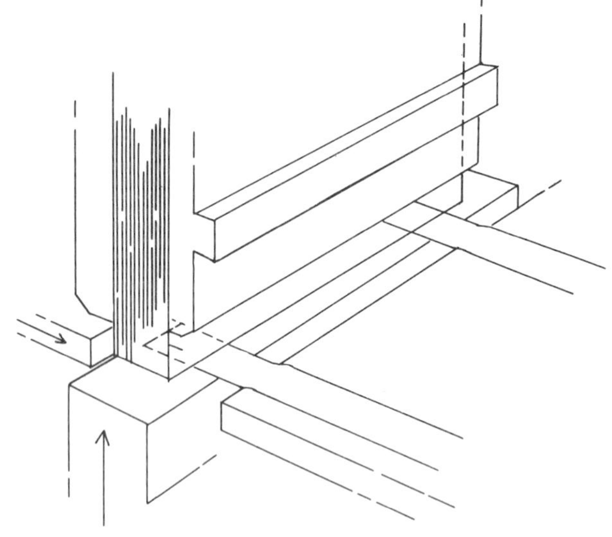

Figure 4.3
Cover breaker setting

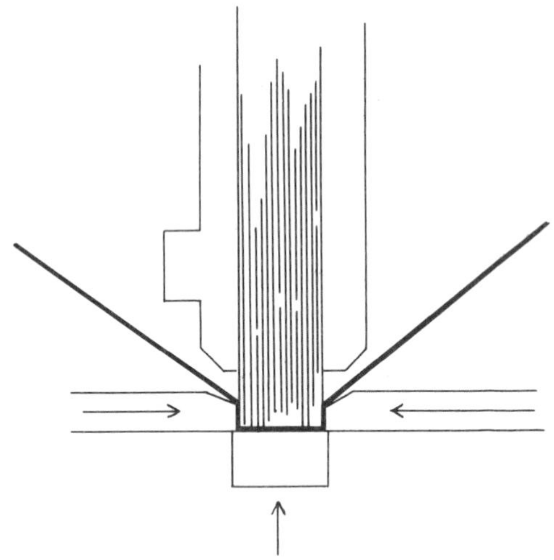

Figure 4.4
Cover breaker unit

block and the backplate. Leave only sufficient room for the cover stock and adhesive. Most machines being built today have an adjustable spine backplate and this should be set so that it supports the spine just before the side nip comes in.

Side-nip blade

The back side-nipping blade should never need adjustment; it must always be in line with the inside edge of the book clamps. In some cases, such as soft pocket-books and directories, it can come outside the back clamp by a mere 0.125 mm, but, however difficult the cover or body stock is, the back side-nip blade should never be inside the back clamp, as this will cause a nail head.

Outside nip blade

The outer side blade is adjustable to accommodate varying thicknesses of books: the correct setting is one that gives a square, firm spine with no obvious pump or mechanical strain. An under-nipped book will squeeze down and crease in the three-knife trimmer. Care must be taken to see that the nip plates never go out of parallel, or a wedge-shaped spine will ensue. A compromise on pressure will have to be made when all the signatures have open ends at the head or the tail (especially if the body stock is heavy). The cover breaker should not be used as a book smasher but only to form the shape of the spine. If a side-gluing unit is in use then the side-nip plates must be of sufficient depth to flatten the side glue and to form it into thin ribbons.

Conveying system

Books being released from the clamps should be transported on their spines for as long as possible. They should then be laid down gently by using variable-speed conveying systems; close laying-down or shingling will increase the cooling time before the three-knife trimmers. Enough cooling time must be allowed, especially when a new bindery layout is being planned, so that even with the softest of papers the adhesive becomes firm enough to withstand the pressures of the trimming clamp.

If wings are fitted to direct the book into the conveying system, make sure that they are firmly close and square, but not so tight as to impede movement, and check that the delivery belt is square so that the book is not distorted. This is especially important when books are being bound with emulsions.

Shrink wrapping

Always take care when shrink wrapping straight from the binding and trimming line, especially if any volatile solvents are left in the print. These will, of course, be entrapped in the block of books swathed in plastic film. Tests should be made before proceeding with long runs to make sure that the heat from the hotmelt and from the shrink-wrapping tunnel does not affect any surface coating of the book cover.

Solvent resistance

Many producers of pocket-books require a hotmelt with solvent resistance built into it. This is because of the amount of solvent in the form of white spirit or paraffin that is left in the very absorbent paper that tends to be used in pocket-books. In fact, any book that is printed with large amounts of ink with a solvent carrier will smell quite strongly and it is then advisable to run checks on the solvent resistance that may be required.

Typical problems with solvent resistance do not show themselves for at least three to six months, whereupon cover adhesion fails, partially or completely, leaving a smooth, waxy surface on the hotmelt film and no adhesive at all on the stock cover. Generally, page strengths are also affected, but any book block will be weaker as soon as the cover is lost.

Caution There are degrees of solvent resistance. We have yet to see a one-shot hotmelt that is totally solvent resistant, so it is essential that you test and find the level of resistance you require. You must test thoroughly any product submitted and this will apply every time you change your ink, your supplier, or your production methods, including your operators' practices when cleaning down or adding solvents to the ink.

Figure 4.5
Cover sander

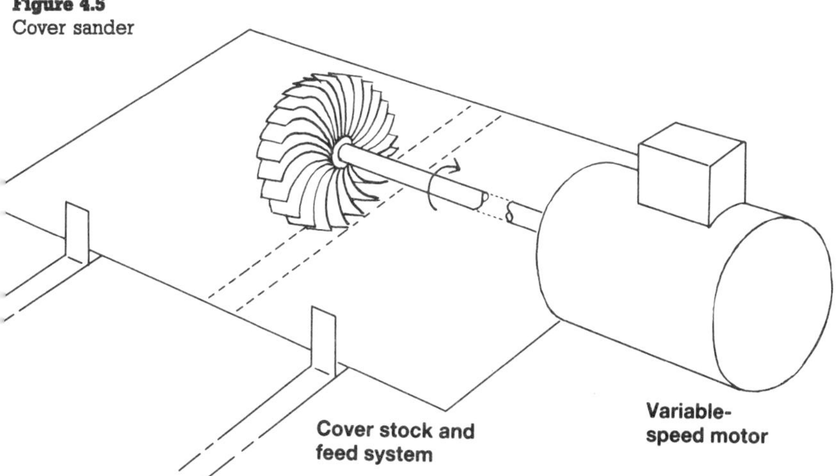

Cover sander

This employs a Black & Decker-type abrasive flap wheel. Kiss-contact removes varnish, clay coatings or ink. It can only be fitted to stream-feed units (Figure 4.5).

Polyurethane (PUR) or reactive hotmelt application (Figure 4.6)

Unlike traditional hotmelts these products are delivered in sealed containers such as a metal 20 kg drum or a sleeve-in-tube system. They are moisture cured, so it is important that the packaging medium not only transports the material safely but also protects it from air and moisture.

Pre-melting

The drum, or slug in its sleeve, is put into a drum unloader that melts and pumps the adhesive. Feeding the binder automatically helps to eliminate any contact with moisture in the air. These moisture-curing products have to be treated with caution and care–not only will they give a

Figure 4.6
PUR tank setting

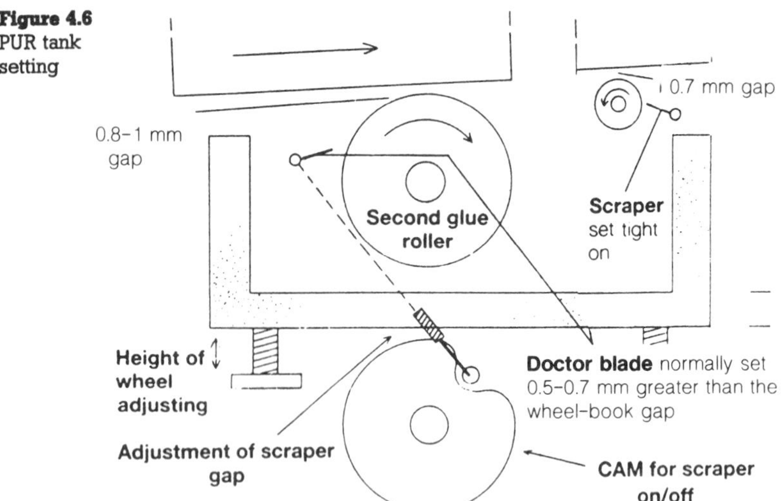

All gaps are measured on a dry application roller.

permanent bond to metal, but at present they contain small quantities of organic isocyanates (MDI). Some older PURs had very short pot lives, low tack and extended trim times, whereas reactive hotmelts are a generation ahead.

Requirements to run with PUR/reactive hotmelt:

1 Special coated hotmelt tank with double thermostatic controls.

2 Good extraction unit for both the hotmelt unit and the drum unloader pre-melter.

3 Well maintained binding machine, as coating weights are quite low.

Starting to run a two-wheel and spinner tank:

1 Set the adhesive running temperature at, and never above, that recommended by the supplier.

2 Set the glue rollers as follows: the first 0.125 mm from the spine; the second 1.5mm maximum and the spinner 0.6-0.7 mm. This should leave you a film of 0.25 mm-0.35 mm on the book spine if the spinner scraper is clean.

One-wheel and spinner tanks:

1 The gap between the book block and the wheel should be set to 1 mm and the spinner 0.7 mm.

Spine preparation:

1 Sanding disc for normal papers.

2 Low notch and sanding disc for difficult stock.

3 Always have sharp notchers and clean the sanding disc regularly with water and a stiff bristle brush.

Cover station:

1 This should be set to give high pressure on the spine, especially when using a one-wheel pot.

2 Books should be seen to rise slightly as the cover station comes up.

3 Short covers will allow PUR to get onto the backup plate. Set off/on scrapers with care.

Operators' book tests:

1 When a book is cold, carefully tear off the front and back cover and inspect for holes.

2 Cut down the spine with a sharp clean knife and inspect for lack of bubbles.

3 Measure the film thickness; it should be no lower than 0.2 mm and no higher than 0.4 mm.

4 Make sure the knife blade is clean before cutting another book, as dirty, blunt blades pull the glue film and will give you a false reading and picture.

5 Moisture content, paper and atmosphere will determine the time to page pull, normally 4-12 hours.

General:

1 Reactive hotmelts will run at high speeds due to its high tack.

2 Reactive hotmelts will trim cleanly within one minute.

3 PURs are normally slower and require a longer trim time.

5 Multi-shot applications

The reasons for using multi-shot applications of hotmelt adhesive are as follows:

1 To produce a book block with the minimum of spine preparation so that one gets, even with the most difficult of paper, an open, flat format. The primer hotmelt is therefore a flexible product with a much lower viscosity, which wets out the smallest undulation after the spine preparation, while the second, higher-viscosity adhesive holds up the lining or book cover stock.

2 For mail order catalogues where extremely high page pulls and flexes are required, a low-viscosity primer is used to flow into the deep notches followed by a second hotmelt placed as a firming medium to hold up the cover.

The settings of the glue rollers are illustrated in Figure 5.1. The aims are the following:

1 The primer tank is to make sure that the low-viscosity hotmelt wets out the paper stock, or flows into the notch, or in the case of burst binding goes into the slot or burst as high as possible.

2 The second application is to lay on an even film to accept the lining material, a stiffening board, or the cover stock. If this is to be a middle shot then it is generally advisable for it to have a higher tack than the final shot which is to draw up the cover stock.

3 Due to higher adhesive performance, the three-shot system is almost obsolete; the two-shot system that has taken its place does not require lining paper or board.

4 Since writing and typesetting a development has taken place and moved from the laboratory. It has been patented and tested at a machine manufacturers plant

Figure 5.1
Adhesive applicator roller settings: hotmelt primer, multi-coat/emulsion primer and emulsion top coat

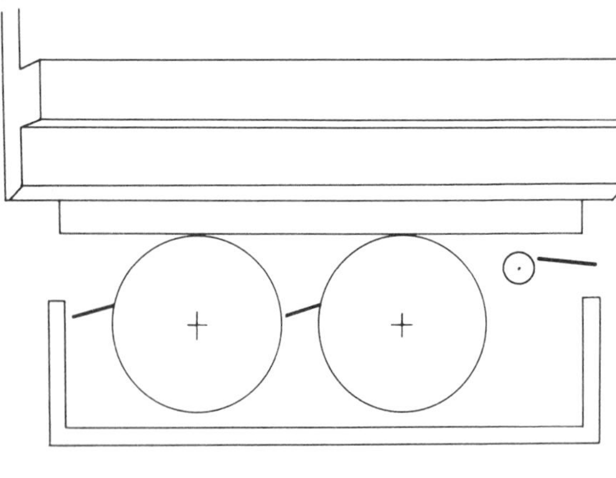

Hotmelt primer setting
Both wheels close. Film thickness controlled with the spinner

Second- or third-shot hotmelt
The aim is to lay on to the primer. Thickness controlled with the spinner

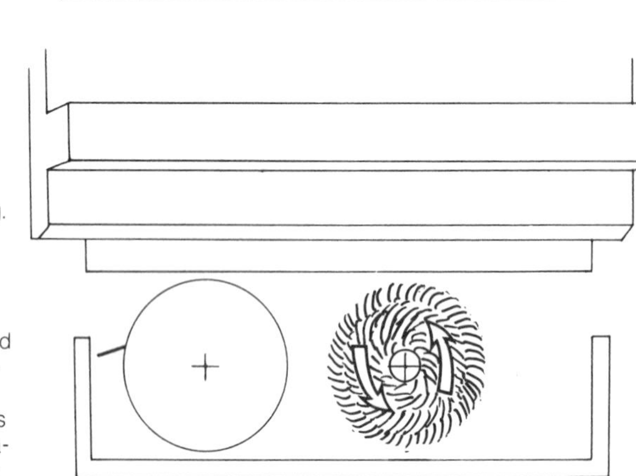

Emulsion primer
Both wheels just kissing. Apply 0.125 mm wet adhesive. Improved primer application may be found when the second roller is replaced by a brush contra rotating. The new two-shot reactive system requires a foam covered application roller and the brush

Figure 5.1 (cont.)

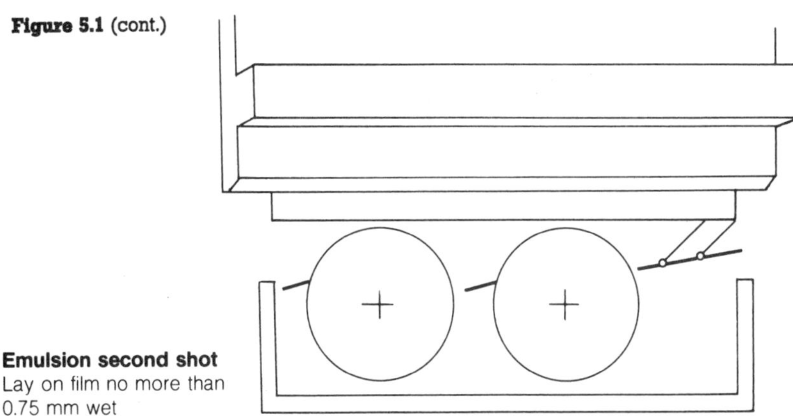

Emulsion second shot
Lay on film no more than 0.75 mm wet

in Switzerland. The new patented innovation is a two-shot emulsion/hotmelt system with an aqueous hardener. Production entails adding the catalyst to the specially formulated emulsion and applying the adhesive via a foam covered application roller. Drying is by infrared two or more metres in length. The special compatible hotmelt top coat is applied from a traditional hotmelt glue tank. End performance indicates it has enhanced page strength combined with a greatly retained round, for hard case books.

Emulsion-hotmelt tank settings (Twinflex system)

The Twinflex is a sophisticated system of binding that uses, in an adapted machine, a special emulsion that binds the papers together and a compatible hotmelt to give strength to the book block or the book and to hold up the cover or lining material. This system of binding has many advantages over any other, as the spine preparation does not require notching, but only the use of a sanding disc, or a means of imparting a fluffy texture to the spine, which thus enables the special emulsion to penetrate into the paper stock. This system of binding gives the best of both worlds inasmuch as one gets the deep penetration and fibre anchorage of an emulsion and the high speed of a hotmelt.

The adaptation of the equipment means that the

emulsion, once applied, is dried by gas heaters, which simultaneously increase the spine temperature to over 80 °C. The warm, dry spine then has a compatible hotmelt adhesive applied to it which is generally of a flexible nature, so that the book can either have a cover drawn on it or a lining paper and then be rounded and backed.

Caution The emulsion and the hotmelt must be completely compatible. The primer emulsion must not foam and must wet out the paper stock immediately. It must not have ingredients that age or migrate. The compatibility of bond between the emulsion and the hotmelt must not break down under extreme conditions of cold crack or high heat resistance. The weakest part of the book should be the cover material or the pages and not the primer-hotmelt adhesion.

Humidification

Because of the heat required in drying the primer adhesive, moisture will have been lost from some or all of the book, so tests should not be carried out until the moisture has once more become even throughout the book and any lost in the binding process regained.

Caution Hotmelt will not bond on to wet emulsion. The primer adhesive has to be completely dry and hot; there is no compatibility between a wet emulsion and a hotmelt.

The setting of non-radiant gas burners

These should be set so that when in operation the wire gauze covering each burner (the gap in the gauze must not be greater than 10 mm) glows cherry-red. The minimum gap between the gas plate and the spine of the book (Figure 5.2) should be between 40 and 80 mm.

If the binding machine has been fitted with baffles then these should always be used to direct the heat on to the spine of the book, as this will help to dry the outer edges where the emulsion may have crept round. The baffles should also be used to protect the rest of the machine from excessive heat. Some large binding machines do not

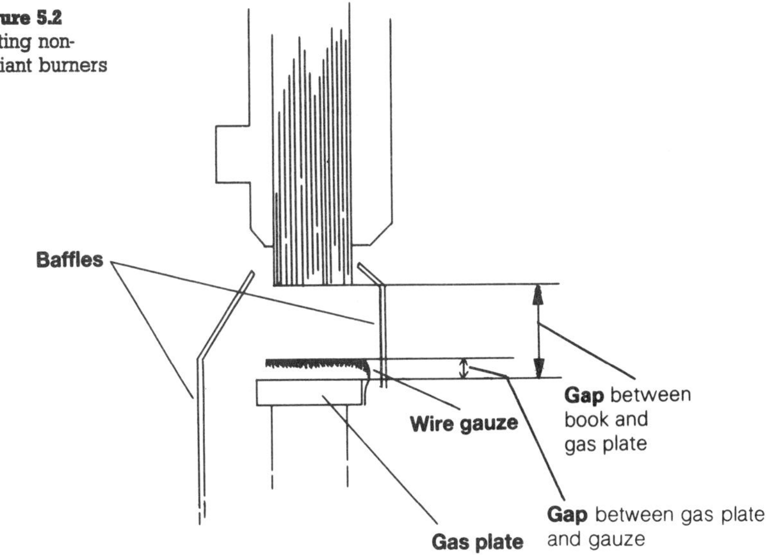

Figure 5.2 Setting non-radiant burners

have baffles fitted but have a curved manifold dryer that fits around the 180° curve of the binding machine. This system dries the edges of book blocks most efficiently.

RF- and HF-assisted drying

The use of radio-frequency (RF) drying in the bindery is now quite commonplace. However, it is important to realize that the right kind of adhesive must be used, so that when the spine adhesive on the book is heated by the vibration of the molecules it does not lose its tack and grip on its cover or lining material, since this will entail a further operation of rubbing down the spine, or of stacking the book on the spine to regain adhesion.

RF and HF generally take the temperature of the spine adhesive up above 65 °C; before trimming, a heat loss of some 40 °C must be seen and a general firming of the adhesive must take place. This can be speeded up by the use of cold air blasts and by moving the books through several pressing units.

Caution If the emulsion is not allowed to penetrate or is not pushed into the paper stock sufficiently before the book enters the stray field then page adhesion can be lost. Tests indicate that if a book is held for 10 seconds before entering an RF field then the page strength is higher than if the book enters immediately after application of the adhesive.

Two-shot emulsion tank settings

The primer tank should be set so that the emulsion is pushed into the paper stock; any excess should be scraped off with a metal scraper bar. The primer should feel tacky after the book has left the first glue tank. If the adhesive feels wet it could be pulled off by the higher viscosity and tack second shot. The second shot of emulsion should be laid on so as to leave sufficient product with enough wet tack to draw up the lining material or cover stock. Side guides should be fitted to both glue tanks, as this reduces flare and adhesive bleed in.

Scraper settings for Twinflex and two-shot emulsion

It is advisable to look closely at the scraper units for both the primer Twinflex system and primer two-shot emulsions (Figure 5.3).

Machines not fitted with scrapers or brush units should be adapted before any tests are conducted with emulsion adhesives.

Endpapering

If any full-production endpapering is to be done, either before or in line, on unsewn binding machines, the choice of an adhesive or adhesive system to bond the endpapers must be given some thought. Because of the subsequent operations, if printed endpapers are used, or if they are bonded to wraprounds or heavily inked areas, then the adhesives must neither affect other materials nor be affected by them.

If hotmelt is to be applied then several points should be noted:

Figure 5.3
Emulsion
scraper setting

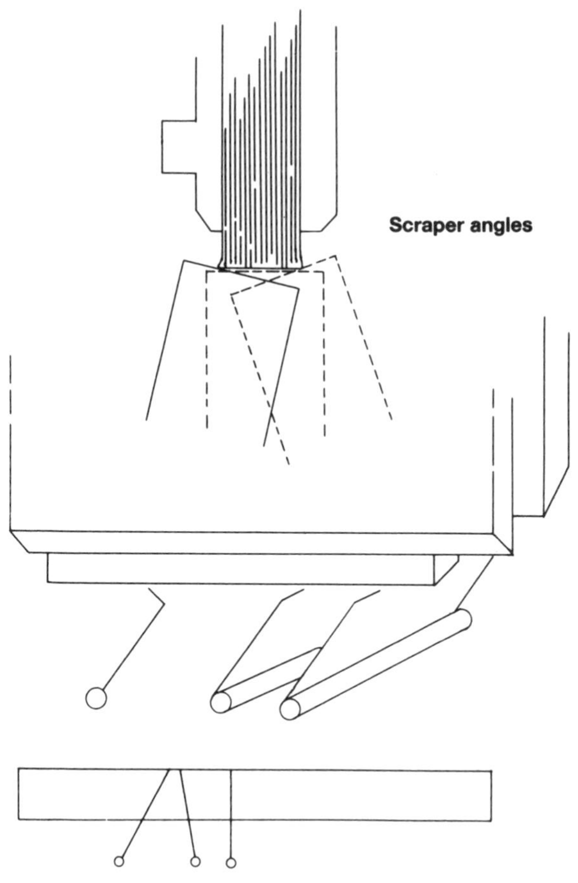

1 The hotmelt film should be pliable enough to be flattened by the subsequent rollers or nip plate.

2 If the hotmelt is firm and forms a ridge then the first and last pages will be damaged during the rounding and backing operation.

3 Care should also be taken that the hotmelt is of a high quality so that it will not be affected by the heated joints during the building-in operation.

4 Emulsions should have sufficient tack to be able to have the endpapers stepped up and to resist slip or twisting.

5 Emulsions should be easy to clean and yet be relatively fast bonding.

Combined endsheets

In the production of these components, the stretch-bind material should be produced so that at least 25–30 per cent stretch can be gained across the width of the spine. The adhesive bonding the endpapers to the centre lining must be pressed completely flat.

When endpapers with step-up ribbons are used in the first and last units on a gathering machine, the ribbons should be innermost so that they come into contact with the first and last signatures. This prevents a build-up or a ridge during the lining operation (Figure 5.4).

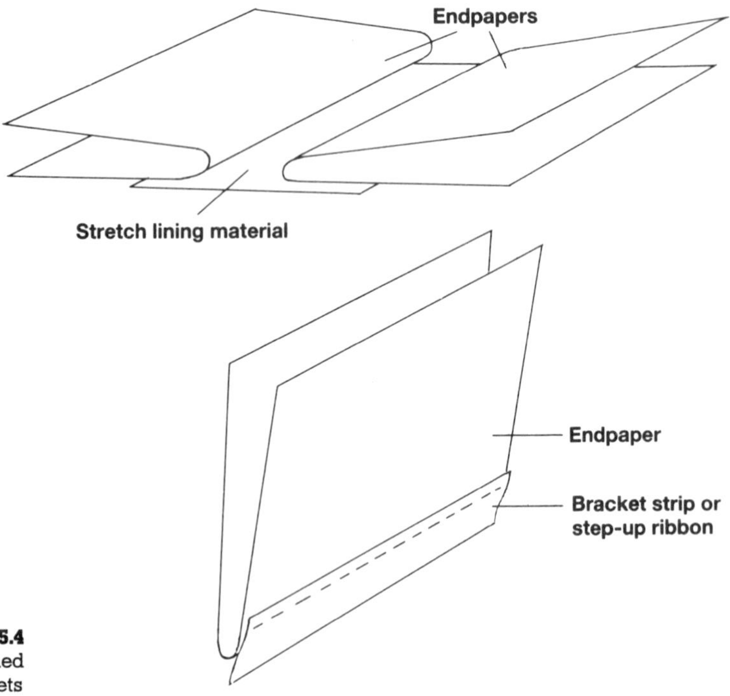

Figure 5.4 Combined endsheets

Adhesives and in-line sewing

Another way of producing a pseudo-sewn book block is to threadseal the signatures before they are placed in the gathering boxes. There are two main systems, the Brehmer Threadsealer and the Petratto cotton thread machine. Both machines stitch an individual section either at or immediately following the last fold on a standard folding machine.

The Brehmer unit uses a sewing thread that incorporates a heat-reactivated double filament and the ends of each stitch are heat-sealed to the fold of the section.

The Petratto machine, on the other hand, uses a standard sewing thread and the individual threads are glued to the spine of the sections with a thin, quick-setting hotmelt. This hotmelt should be of a high standard so that when the main spine adhesive is applied the thin film of hotmelt applied to the threat fuses with the main body of hotmelt that draws on the cover material.

Rounding and backing unsewn book blocks

The production of book blocks on a standard unsewn-binding machine is now commonplace. However, a few points should be noted.

Any adhesive used should have sufficient stretch and a reluctance to shrink back. Hotmelts, for instance, should have an elongation of an adhesive film of at least 100 per cent and the regression should certainly not be more than 30 per cent.

Note also that the stretch crêpe or cloth must have stretchability of more than 30 per cent. These figures are given as a guideline, since every country has its own preference regarding the amount of round that a book should carry. In Britain a book has to have a deep round with heavy shoulders, whereas on the continent books are generally shoulderless with an attractive round.

Round retention can be judged by taking a book block before rounding and drawing a line across the head. After rounding, another line is drawn between the extremities of the original, which should now be curved. Inspecting

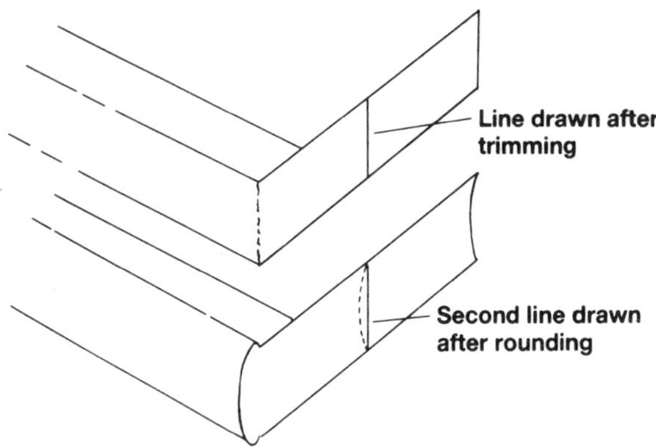

Figure 5.5 Book block round-retention tests

the marks on the head of this test book will show how good or poor the round retention is (Figure 5.5).

Backing materials

Mull Not used in unsewn binding unless it has a stretchable backing material.

Boards Stiff, low-cost material used as the insert and stiffener for flextabil binding.

Crêpe paper Paper that normally has between 25 and 30 per cent stretch, which is required if the book blocks are to be subsequently rounded.

Kraft paper Generally a brown, firm paper used for flat-back, cased-in work. Bleached kraft can be used on the Otabind system.

Liner A coated stretchable linen generally used on more expensive sewn or unsewn book blocks.

6 Other binding techniques

Burst/slotted binding

Burst, slotted or perforated binding is a system whereby a slit or a slot is punched into the paper prior to the last fold (Figure 6.1). The length of this slit will be governed by several factors:

1 The type of adhesive used.

2 The speed of the binding machine.

3 How clean a cut can be made by the folding machine or web press.

Burst/slotted binding has been extremely successful with emulsion adhesives. This is because after the book block is bound, emulsion will carry on moving until completely dry. Other adhesive systems suitable for burst or slotted binding include the Twinflex or emulsion-hotmelt system, provided that after the emulsion has been forced into the slot, the surface adhesive is scraped off and brushed out and sufficient heat is used to dry all the emulsion before the hotmelt is applied to the spine. Two-shot hotmelt systems are also in use with burst binding, using a primer hotmelt of very low-viscosity and long open-time and a higher-viscosity hotmelt that helps to force the primer product well into the slot.

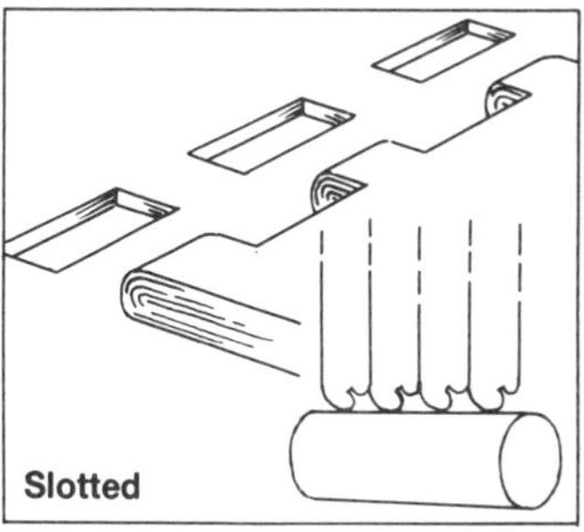

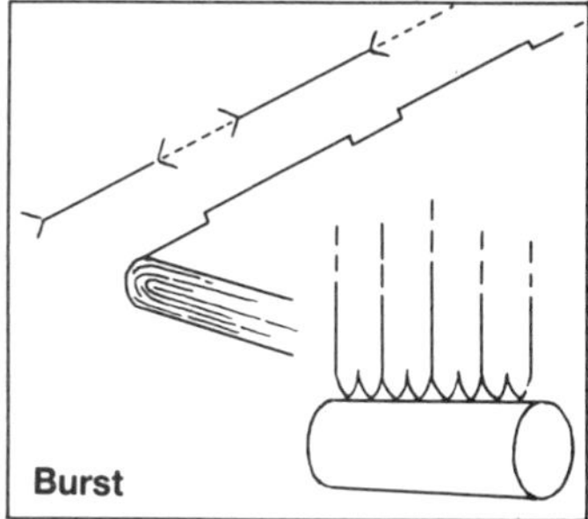

Figure 6.1 Slotted and burst binding

6

Flextabil

This system of binding catalogues was developed many years ago. The bolts or folds down the spine of the book (bolts/folds) are specially cut, leaving between 25 and 30 mm uncut at the head and tail (Figure 6.2). The depth of this cut is deep enough to accept a layer of adhesive and a thin piece of board to act as a stiffener. A final coat of hotmelt is applied to the whole of the spine and the cover board is drawn on. The binding machine has to be specially constructed for this system to work. This is now almost obsolete.

Figure 6.2 Flextabil binding

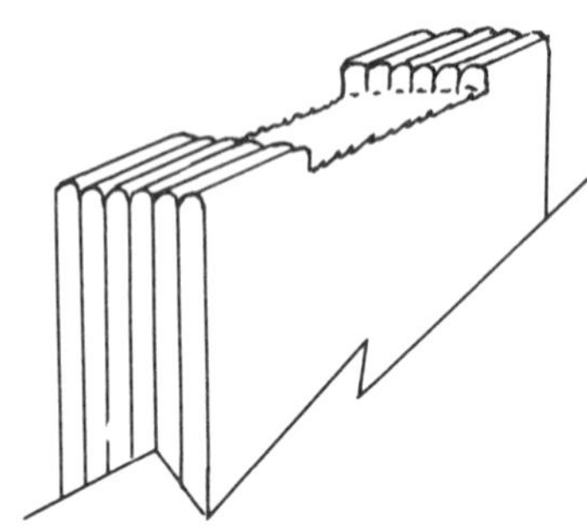

Otabind

This system of binding was developed in Finland and a worldwide patent is claimed for it. The developers have liaised closely with a binding machinery manufacturer who has provided the special equipment. The spine can be cut back, sewn or slotted, and one or two shots of emulsion adhesive (generally one) are applied to the spine. A cloth or crêpe paper is wrapped round the book

Figure 6.3 Otabind system

block and with the aid of a side-gluing unit the crêpe or cloth is attached firmly to the first and last sheets of the book. A further side glue is then applied to the outside of the lining material and finally the cover is drawn up and attached by the side glue only. Indications are that the soft-cover books produced by this means look more attractive than usual, as the spines do not crease or bend as the books are opened. They also have extremely good lay-flat properties (Figure 6.3).

Swiss brochure (Swiss style)

This is similar to the Otabind system in many ways, but only the back section of the spine is attached to the cover. In other words, there is one line of side glue down the length of the book, 1-5 mm in from the spine.

7 Book testing and fault finding

It is essential that the bookbinder carries out some tests on bound books to check for faults.

In the case of emulsion-bound books these must be aged for at least 24 hours. Books produced with hotmelt should be allowed to cool until the spine definitely feels cold.

Useful tests include the following:

1 Slitting the book down through the glue line with a sharp blade; this will show the frequency of notching, the depth, how the glue has or has not penetrated into the notches, and, most importantly, the thickness of the glue layer, which should be 0.5 mm of bubble-free continuous film (Figure 7.1(a)).

2 Stripping off the cover to estimate the cover adhesion, which should not be less than 90 per cent. Wetting the paper left on the adhesive layer makes it possible to see whether the glue layer is smooth with a matt finish, or shiny, the latter indicating that the cover has not been in correct contact with the adhesive.

If the glue layer is honeycombed, bubbled or rigid then look at the fault-finding section at the end of this chapter.

3 Opening a book, placing it on a firm surface and pulling individual pages you will get a rough idea whether the page anchorage is good enough (Figure 7.1(b)).

Figure 7.1 Testing of unsewn books

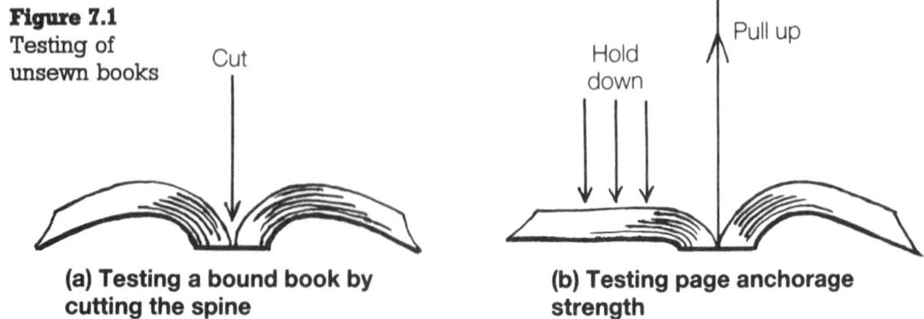

(a) Testing a bound book by cutting the spine

(b) Testing page anchorage strength

National Adhesives Bookbinding Service Report

Confidential

Customer	:	Invoice number	:
Grade used	:	Machine	:
Book title	:	Book length	:

Test carried out		Results	Comments
Page-pull	Front :		
	Centre :		
	Back :		
	Average :		
Flex :			
Page-pull after flex :			
Cold crack :			
Subway :			
Coating weight/ head tail :			
Notches depth :			
Notches separation :			
Appearance :			
Cover adhesion :			
Speed* :			
Spine preparation* :			
Other comments* :			

Time spent performing tests :

Unless otherwise stated these tests will be charged at a rate of £ per hour

* Speed, spine preparation, etc. to be filled in by the operator

Figure 7.2 Adhesive usage and measure

For binderies that have a laboratory facility, further tests are possible, such as heat resistance (the subway test), cold resistance (this measures the cold crack resistance of a book), solvent resistance, page-pull, and flexing. A full list of possible tests is given in Figure 7.2.

Equipment required

Heat resistance test Constant fan oven complete with digital temperature readout.

Cold crack and resistance Refrigerator that can hold ± 1 °C.

Solvent tests Glass tank with sealable lid and a metal frame to hold bonded samples. The tank should be large enough to hold four foil containers which are filled with the offending ink.

Page-pull and flex tests While the flex test is the most important, the equipment is expensive, and not everyone will be able to afford it. The manufacturers of such equipment are:

- Moffett Precision Products, 351 Reed St, PO Box 266, Somerset, Wisconsin 54025, USA;
- PIRA Research Association, Leatherhead, UK;
- Pull-Flex Manufacturing Co., 840 Poplar Lane, Bolingbrook, Illinois 60439, USA;
- Sigloch Maschinenbau GmbH.

Page-pull and flex tests

To set a standard for page-pull and flexing is difficult; there are too many widely varying types of machines in use and several of them are quite unsatisfactory. Variations in pull strengths can be changed simply in the loading of the papers. Some methods require a book to be opened out flat; others pull the page while the book is almost closed. Different units of measurement are also used; these can easily be converted, but it all adds to the confusion.

In the past it was suggested that 4.50 N/cm was a satisfactory pull strength, but now that adhesives have improved a higher standard should be sought:

UK standard

Below 5.00 N/cm	Unacceptable
5.00-7.25 N/cm	Satisfactory
7.25-9.00 N/cm	Good
Above 9.00 N/cm	Very good

German standard

Below 4.50 N/cm	Unacceptable
4.50-6.25 N/cm	Satisfactory
6.25-7.25 N/cm	Good
7.25-8.00 N/cm	Very good
Above 8.00 N/cm	Excellent

USA standard

Below 2.00 lb/in	Unacceptable
2.00-2.50 lb/in	Satisfactory
2.50-3.50 lb/in	Good
3.50-4.00 lb/in	Very good
Above 4.00 lb/in	Excellent

Flex testing

A machine must be able to flex a page through an angle of 110-120°. The page should be subjected to a load of 1 N/cm before flexing begins.

Flexing guide

Magazines	100-150 flexes per page
Pocket-books	200 flexes
Textbooks	250 flexes
Diaries	300 flexes
Catalogues	500-1000 flexes

7

Evaluation of adhesive-bound books made easy

For the evaluation of adhesive-bound books the following features should be tested in the order given:

1 Book appearance

2 Page strength

3 Cover adhesion

4 Adhesive film

If the page-pull values are low and the other features seem right, then check adhesion to the paper stock

5 Spine preparation

6 Grain of paper

Below are the most important points to look at regarding each of these features, and the most common causes of possible faults.

Book appearance

Unsquare spine; wedge-shape glue film; cover register.

Page strength

Minimum values are 5.00 N/cm 100 flexes.

An operator will usually test by hand; to tell a good book from a bad one in this manner requires a great deal of experience.

A reduction in pull strengths can be detected by 20-25 per cent when the grain of the paper runs from spine to foredge. The acceptable page strength level must still remain the same, whatever the paper or the grain.

Cover adhesion

Evaluate the amount of fibre tear as a percentage of the total bond area. This will normally be 100 per cent; if it falls below 90 per cent then something is drastically wrong.

Adhesive film

Check the adhesive coating weight at the head and tail of the book, then split the book along its spine and check all the way along. Coating weight should be 0.5-0.6 mm (0.020-0.024 in).

Spine preparation

Poor spine preparation is the most common cause of a poor book. If the paper stock requires notching then ensure that notches appear 6-8 mm apart and are deep into the page.

Grain of paper

Another point to check is the grain of paper, which should run from head to tail of the book (lengthways). If the paper grain is across the book, lower page-pull values will be obtained as the grain tends to 'spring' the page out at the spine (Figure 7.3).

Figure 7.3 Effect of paper grain on lie of pages

A guide to estimating one-shot adhesive usage

It is no good estimating the amount of adhesive you could use on a particular run, unless your binding machine operator controls the amount, or thickness, of the hotmelt that is laid on the spine.

A magnifying device with a measure attached should be used; a typical device is shown in Figure 7.4.

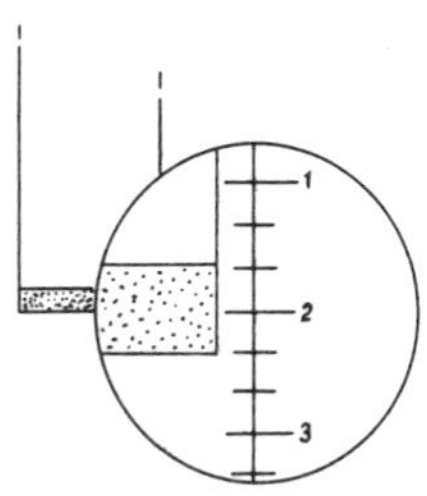

Figure 7.4 Magnifier with measure

The first step is to measure the length, L, of the book before trimming, and the width, W, before cutting off the folds or bolts. Multiplying these together gives us the area of the spine, and multiplying this in turn by the average thickness, T, of the hotmelt gives us the volume of adhesive required. This in its turn has only to be multiplied by the density, D, to give us the mass, M, of adhesive per book. Thus

$$\textit{Mass} = \textit{Length} \times \textit{Width} \times \textit{Thickness} \times \textit{Density}$$

or for short:

$$M = LWTD$$

As an example, let us take a book length of 300 mm and a width of 50 mm before trimming or cutting, and a normal average hotmelt thickness of 0.5 mm. Let us say that the density of the hotmelt is one gram per cubic centimetre (a fairly general figure), or one gram per thousand cubic millimetres. Then

$$\text{Mass } (M) = 300\ (L) \times 50\ (W) \times 0.5\ (T) \times \frac{1}{1000}\ (D)$$

$$= 7.5 \text{ grams per book}$$

Fault finding—spine gluing

Adhesive running in

Causes: book low in clamp; cover drum too high; excess glue on front wheel; first wheel too hard on book; incorrect height of cover station; check also if run-ins are between badly folded signatures. The end result is a mousetrap opening with poor appearance (Figure 7.5).

Figure 7.5 Adhesive running in

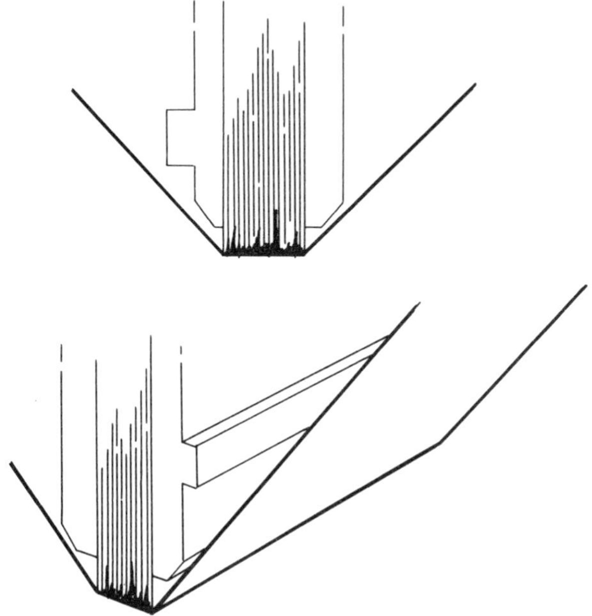

Book not square

Causes: roughing disc not level; backup disc or backup plate not parallel with the inside clamp; not enough adhesive on first or last few pages. The end result is poor adhesion on the immediate inside pages and a one-sided nail head (Figure 7.6).

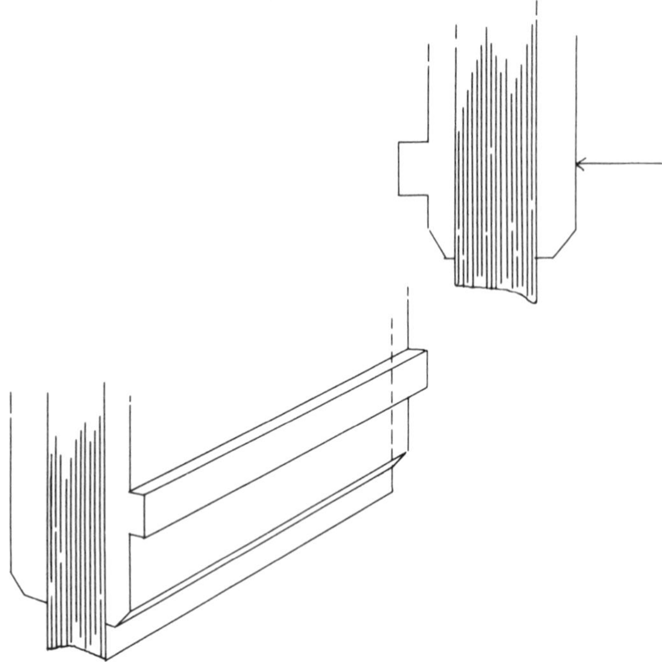

Figure 7.6
Book not square

Cavity spine

Causes: cover breakers too tight; blunt knife or roughener; roughener with too great a tilt. The end result is poor cover adhesion and chipping on trimming (Figure 7.7).

Figure 7.7
Cavity spine

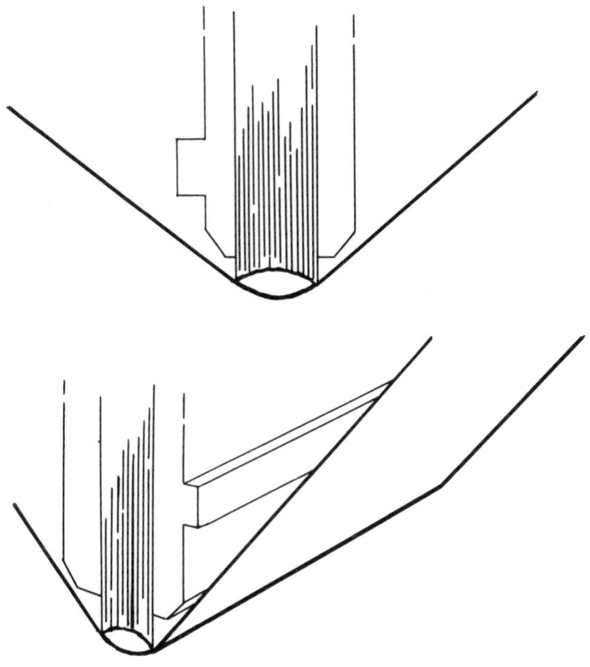

Chip-out at the head

Causes: knife needs resharpening; incorrect knife speed; incorrect outside disc pressure. The end result is an unattractive appearance of the head with chipping on trimming (Figure 7.8).

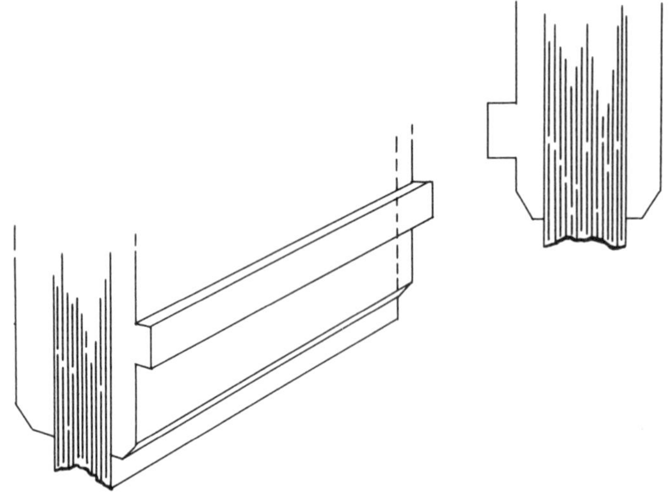

Figure 7.8 Chip-out at the head

Concave spine

Causes: cover breakers too tight. The end result is poor stacking, and an unattractive spine (Figure 7.9).

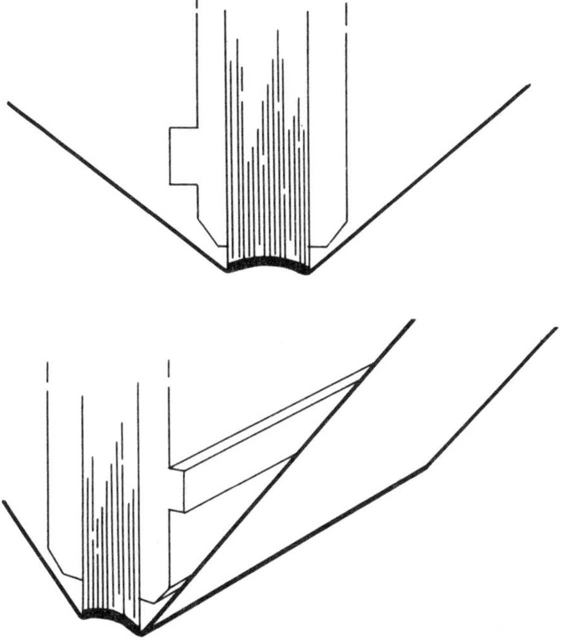

Figure 7.9
Concave spine

Cover register

Check: cover feed; raceway; suction pads; drive rollers. The end result is an unacceptable finished book with the book title running off (Figure 7.10).

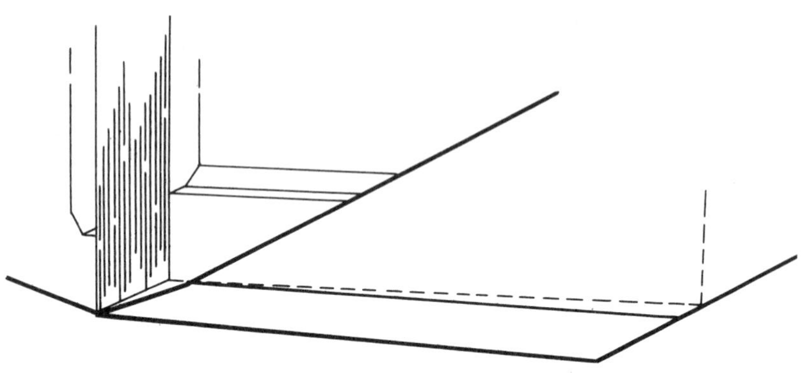

Figure 7.10
Cover register

Feather on book back

Causes: adhesive and/or spinner temperature too low; wrong spinner height; dirty spinner; worn scraper on spinner. The end result is poor cover adhesion and an unattractive spine (Figure 7.11).

Figure 7.11
Feather on book back

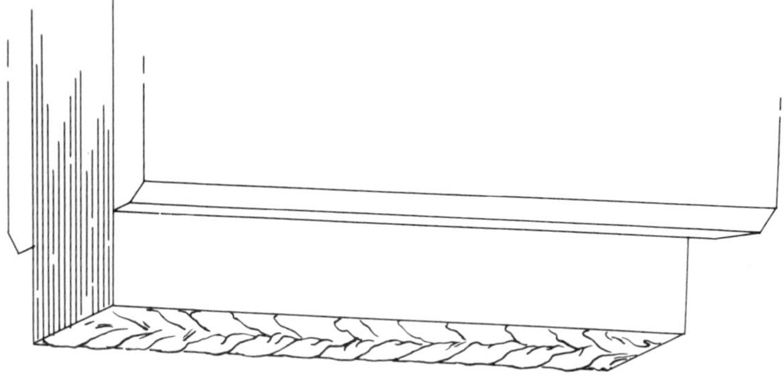

Gaps in glue film before the cover station

Causes: wrong running temperature; wrong spinner temperature; dirty spinner; scraper worn on spinner; wrong adhesive level in pot; dirt under wheel scraper. The end result is cover wrinkle, poor cover adhesion, and poor trimming (Figure 7.12).

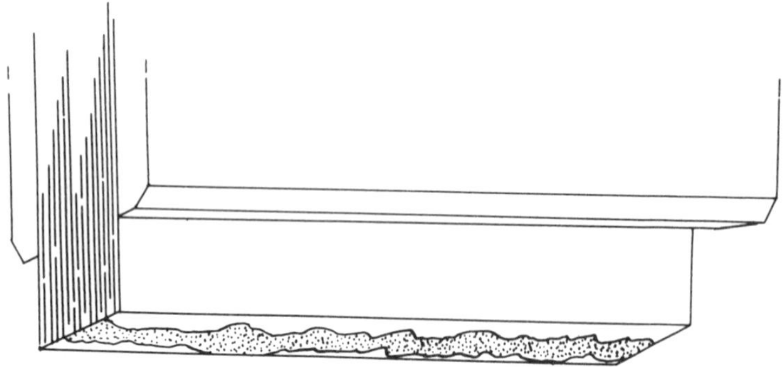

Figure 7.12
Gaps in glue film before the cover station

Holes in glue film

Causes: insufficient glue applied; book too tight in clamp; cover station not raised high enough; maladjusted timing of cover station and side nip (spine not being held as side nip exerts pressure); cold spinner; wrong glue temperature; wrong open time of hotmelt. The end result is poor heat and cold crack resistance (Figure 7.13).

Figure 7.13
Holes in glue film

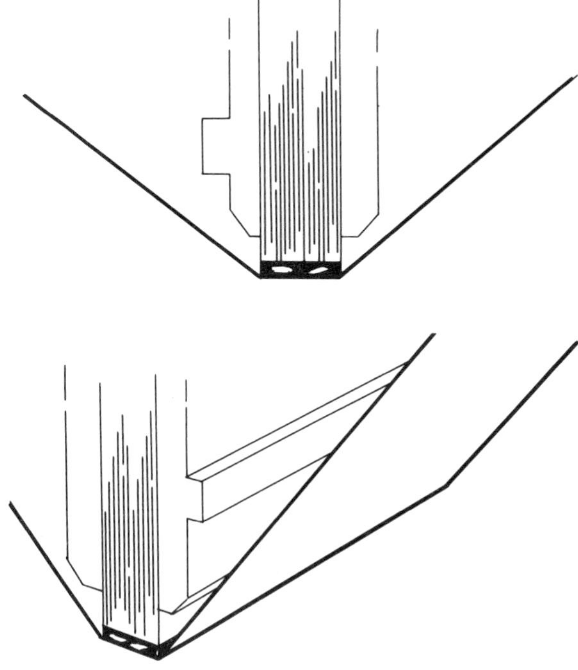

Honeycomb film

Causes: moisture in cover or book stock; wrong glue temperature; wrong spinner temperature; wrong level of the adhesive in pot. The end result is poor page strength, poor heat resistance, and poor cold crack (Figure 7.14).

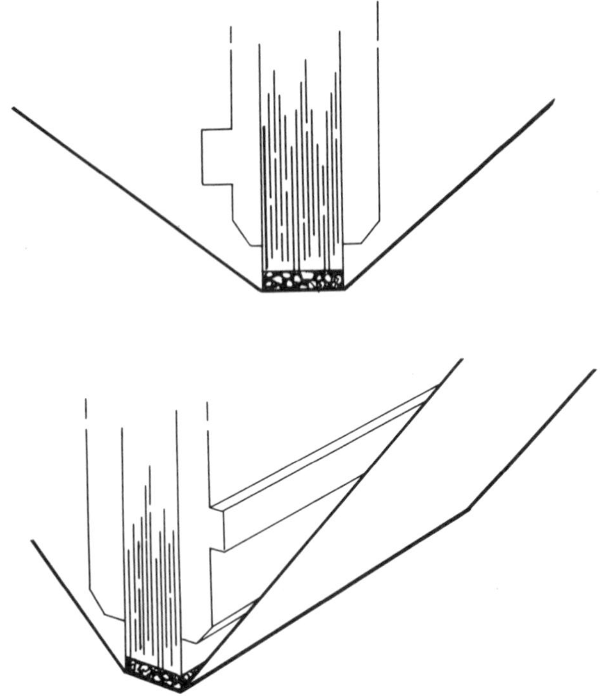

Figure 7.14 Honeycomb film

Insufficient adhesive

Check: level of adhesive in tank; glue roller settings; scrapers; temperature of spinners; spinners' gap setting. The end result is poor page strength, poor cold crack, poor heat resistance, and poor cover adhesion (Figure 7.15).

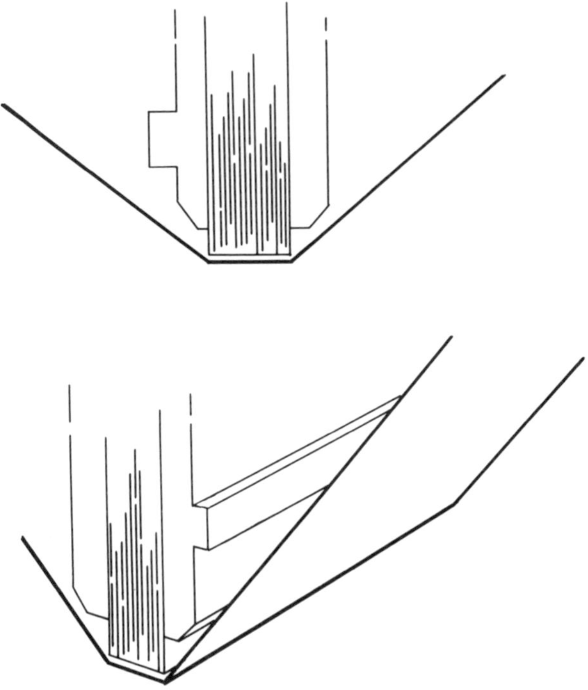

Figure 7.15 Insufficient adhesive

Inverted spine preparation

Causes: clamp drops as the book passes over the spine cutting unit. The end result is cover adhesion head and tail with a bubble or crease in the centre, reduction in page-pull strength. Check clamp bearings, track wear, cutting unit alignment (Figure 7.16).

Figure 7.16
Inverted spine

Mushroom spine

Causes: book low in clamp; cover drum and/or backup plate too high; adhesive application wheels too high; wrong height of cover station. The end result is problems in trimming and stacking (Figure 7.17).

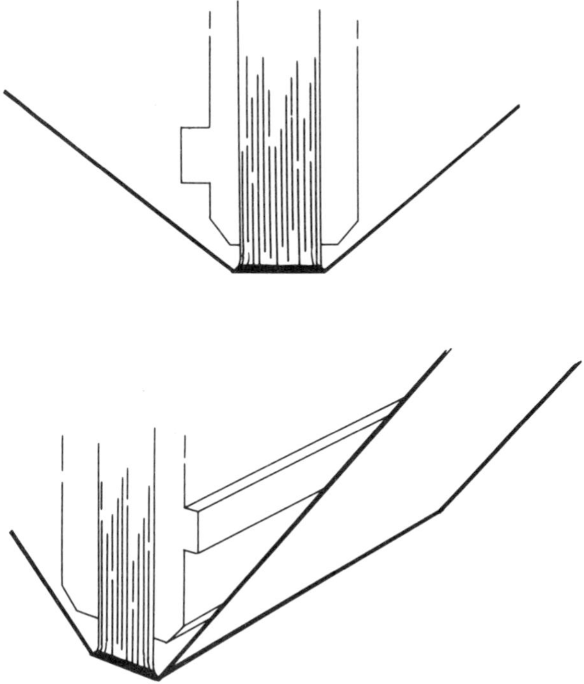

Figure 7.17 Mushroom spine

Nail head

Check: cover drum height; cover breakers; height of backup plate. The end result is difficulty when trimming and chipping on varnished cover stock (Figure 7.18).

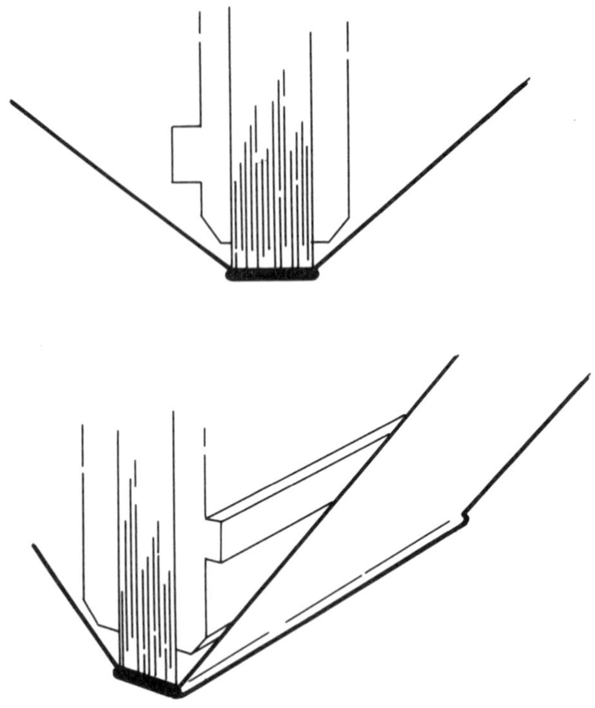

Figure 7.18
Nail head

Rails on uneven cover

Causes: book high in clamp. Remedies: lower rougheners and bring up cover station. The end result is poor cover adhesion in the centre and an unattractive spine (Figure 7.19).

Figure 7.19
Rails on uneven cover

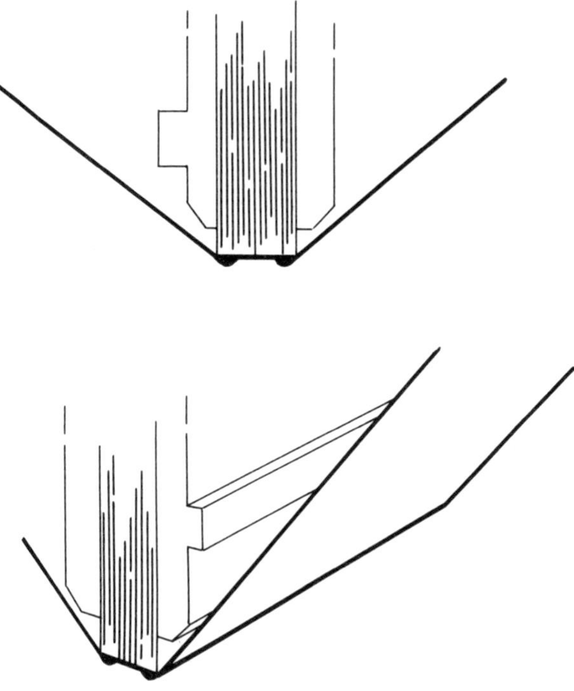

Rough edge before adhesive is applied

Remedies: sharpen roughers; reduce roughening; check roughening backup plate; check the backup friction disc is in line with the inside book clamp. The end result is poor inside page adhesion and a one-sided nail head (Figure 7.20).

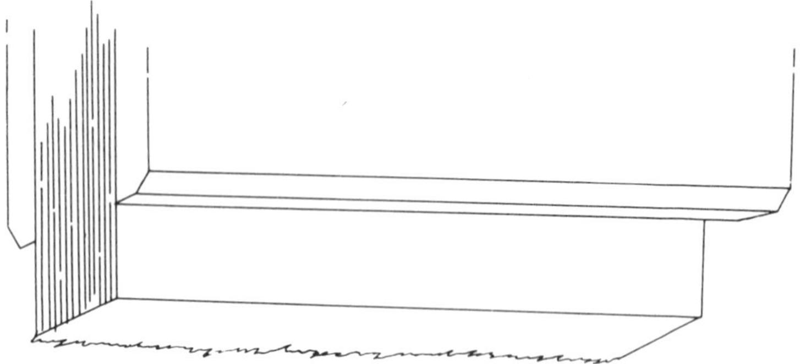

Figure 7.20 Rough edge before adhesive is applied

Round spine

Check: adhesive coating weight; cover breakers; clamp pressure; score stiff covers. The end result is poor page-pull front and back and poor appearance (Figure 7.21).

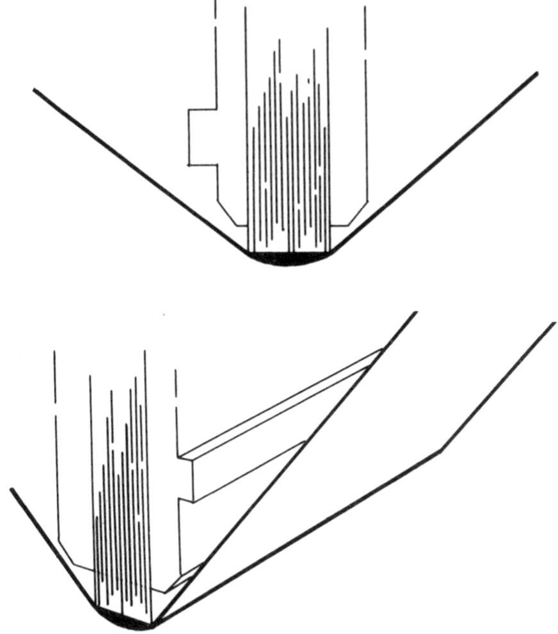

Figure 7.21
Round spine

Uneven glue line

Causes: insufficient adhesive applied or spinner too low; poor hotmelt; dropping in viscosity on degrading; second roller too low–adhesive floods as scraper opens. The end result is poor cover adhesion and poor page strength (Figure 7.22).

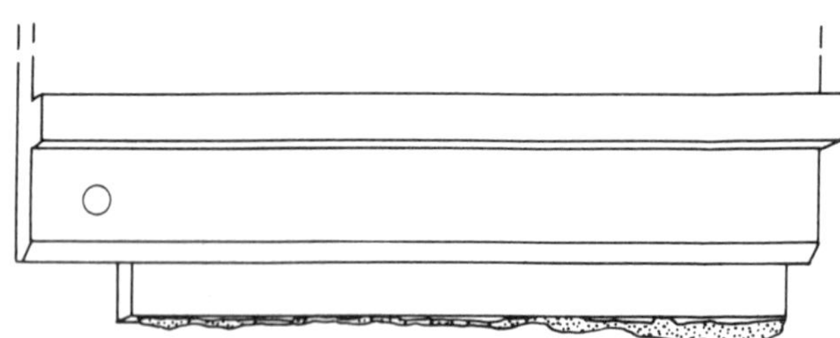

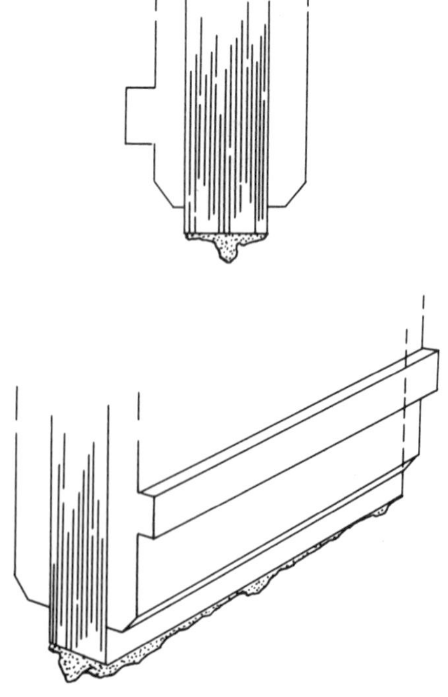

Figure 7.22 Uneven glue line

Wedge adhesive coating across book

Causes: spinner not true; glue unit out of level. The end result is one side with poor cover adhesion and the outside pages with poor page-pull (Figure 7.23).

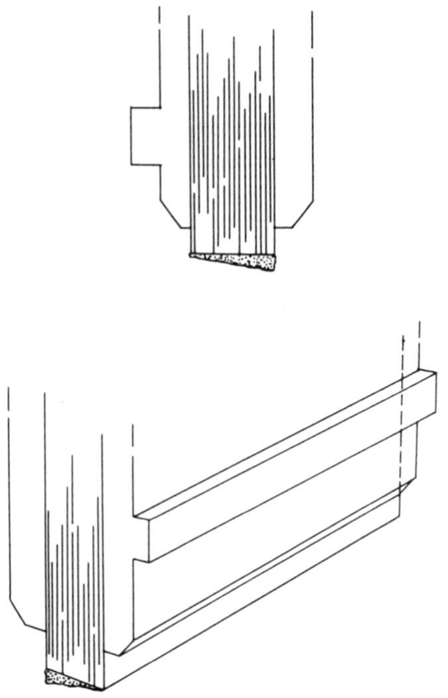

Figure 7.23 Wedge adhesive coating across book

Wedge film

Wedge film from head to tail: causes: clamp pressure too low (book has slipped in clamp); cover station not true. The end result is an unattractive book with poor page strength at the head or tail (Figure 7.24).

Figure 7.24
Wedge film

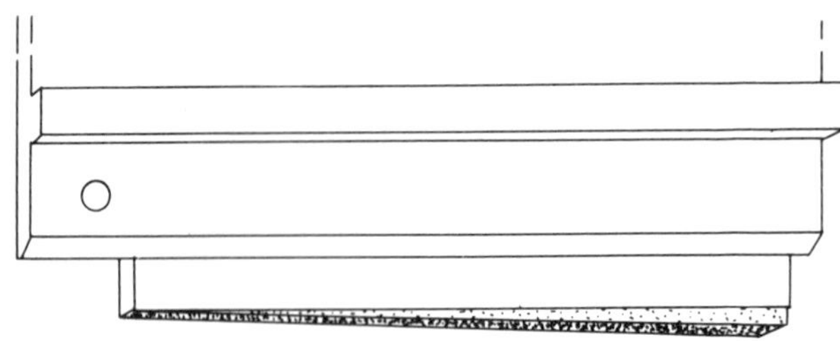

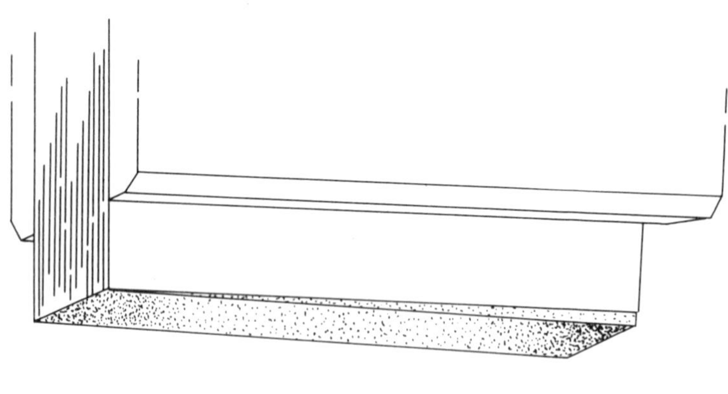

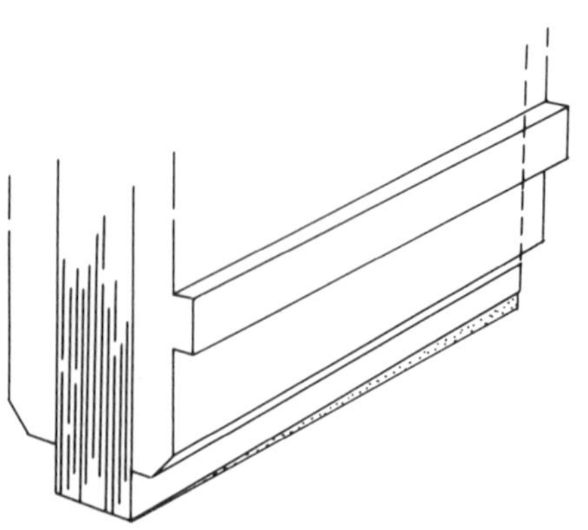

Wideback or flair

Causes: roughening disc not parallel with clamp; backing plate on roughening incorrectly set. The end result is an unattractive spine and problems in stack trimming (Figure 7.25).

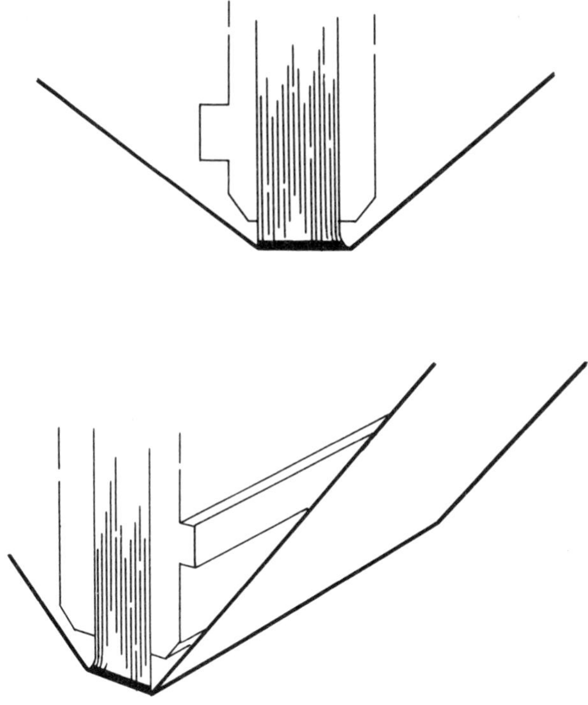

Figure 7.25 Wideback or flair

Wrinkled cover

Causes: book too high in clamp; rougheners too high; loose cover; cover station too low. The end result is an unattractive spine, poor trimming, and an unreadable title (Figure 7.26).

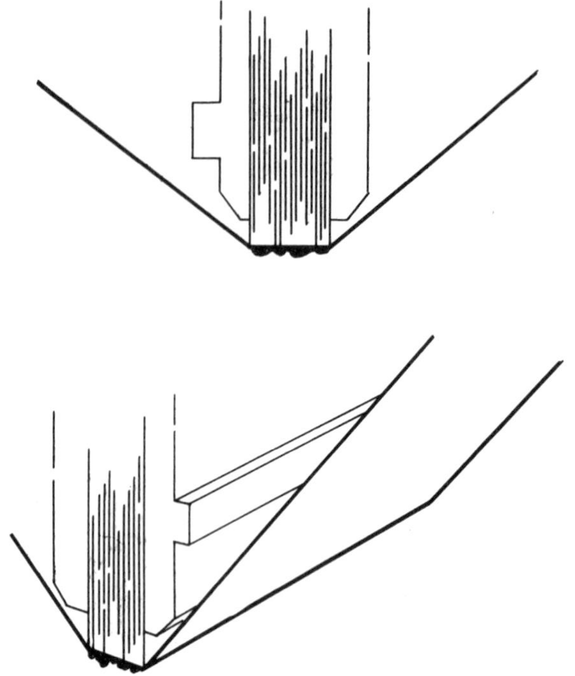

Figure 7.26 Wrinkled cover

Fault finding–side gluing

Bonded to one side only

This has to be a mechanical problem. Causes: nip unit setting; cover plate and side nip timing or back nip bar/plate not in line with the inside of the back clamp (Figure 7.27).

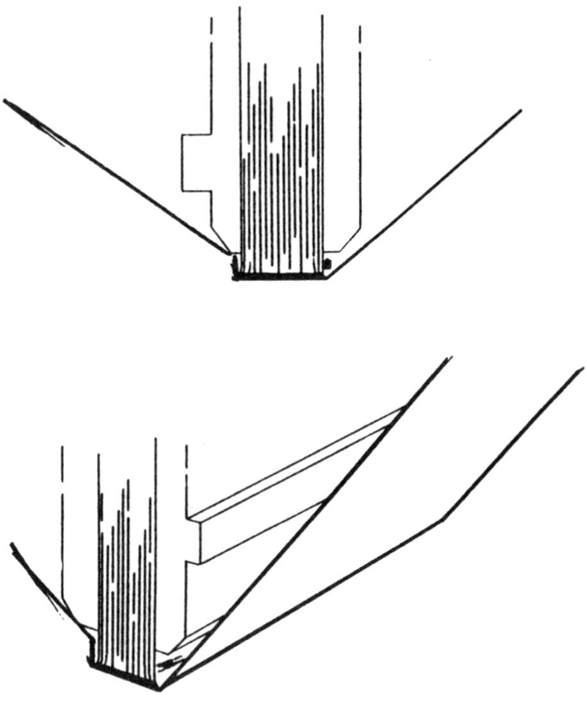

Figure 7.27
Bonded to one side only

Cobwebbing around the machine

Remedies: check viscosity and running temperature; reduce application thickness (Figure 7.28).

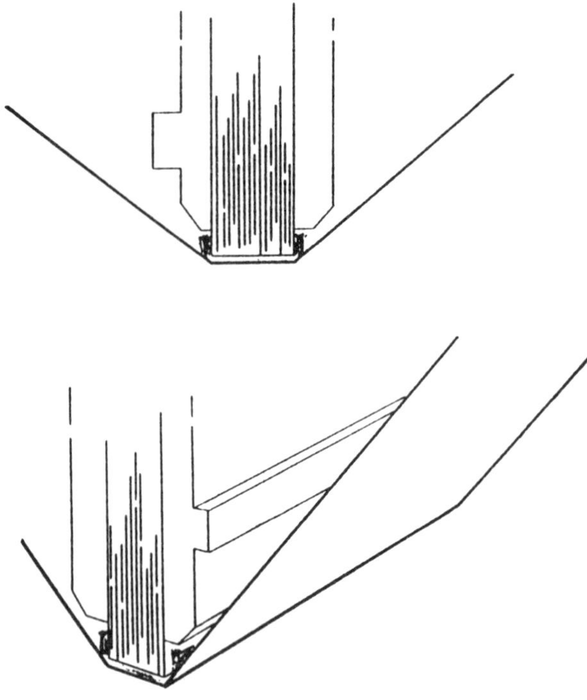

Figure 7.28 Cobwebbing around the machine

Side glue not flattened

Causes: side glue applicators set too high for the depth of the nip plates/bars. Remedies: fit deeper nip bars; increase nip pressure; check temperature or open time of adhesive. The end result is a swollen spine, difficulty in pile trimming, and crush marks on the book spine (Figure 7.29).

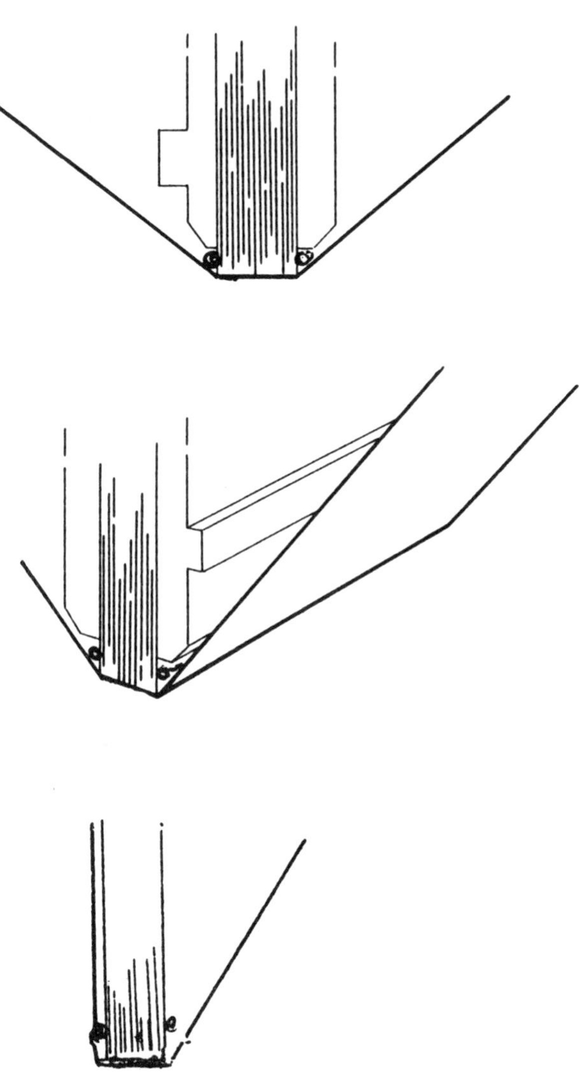

Figure 7.29 Side glue not flattened

Spine smearing/guillotine blade contamination

Causes: too much side glue being used or the adhesive is pressure sensitive. Remedy: find a high-tack low-viscosity product with a shorter open time (Figure 7.30).

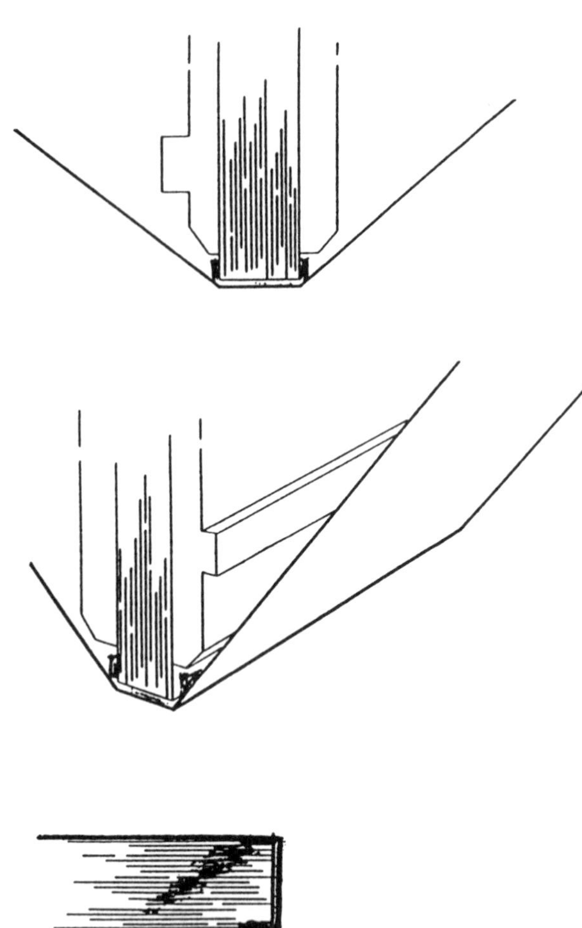

Figure 7.30 Spine smearing/ guillotine blade contamination

Trouble shooting guide on paper problems for the bookbinder

Cockling or wavy edges Over-dried paper will steadily increase its relative humidity, thus the paper will grow. Keep drying temperatures as low as possible; re-moisten on the press.

Cracking at the fold Over-dried with intense heat, enbrittles the coating medium. Re-moisten where possible or use a water line.

Fibre lift Mechanical fibres that contain lignin expand under heat; this can give glossy papers a rougher surface. Keep drying temperatures low. Ask the buyer to choose wood-free paper.

Poor page strength Good results one week, poor results the next and yet bound on the same machine, same adhesive, and operator. Intense drying makes the fibres brittle, i.e. LWC paper is 50 per cent mechanical pulp and 50 per cent wood-free. Brittleness in the groundwood can reduce the page flex and pull strength by half.

Stepping after trimming Over-dried and mixed paper stocks. Growth will vary in speed and amount due to the relevant humidity. Keep drying temperatures to a minimum, re-moisten on the press, and do not use mixed papers.

Spine damage after the trimming operation

Spine crease Spongy spine. Increase nip pressure on the binding machine. Check guillotine clamp pressure. Investigate the grinding angle of blade. Test for damp cover board due to aqueous inks or varnishes. Monitor board delamination and test other boards on the same work.

8 Endpapering and lining

Hand-tipped work is performed by brushing out several inserts or endpapers at a given time. The adhesive has to be brushable and slow, so that the product is still open or wet until the substrates are combined.

Emulsions and pastes with emulsions

On the older endpaper machines with a wheel applicator that forms part of the pot, the only thing that stops the adhesive dripping out is the thixotropic nature of the product. When the agitation stops, the adhesive starts to thicken up, which reduces any tendency to flow. Starch pastes or emulsion-paste blends are generally quite slow in drying; this helps to give good deep bonds if the materials bond easily. The main problem with pastes is their low solids content and the amount of water that must be present in the paper stock.

Emulsions are used for more difficult endpapers and body stocks, and on faster machinery with extrusion equipment. They also offer increased insurance of a deeper bond. The emulsion should be low in viscosity so that it pumps well and tends less to block in the small-diameter piping through which the adhesive is pumped. Low-viscosity should be combined with high solids content to reduce the amount of water passing into the body stock. Emulsions do not generally perform well on densely inked areas, especially with oil-bound inks, which tend to bleed if they wet at all; hotmelt adhesives are used for these difficult papers.

Hotmelts

Endpapering and tipping machines adapted for the use of hotmelts can run at very high speeds. The adhesion on to over-inked papers or wraprounds is extremely good. Hotmelts do not contain water, so they assist in reducing any cockle or waviness in the paper.*

Take care that the hotmelt is of a high standard, so that no oil leaches out over the period of months. The film should be flexible to ensure that it can be flattened by the pressure rollers and that during the rounding and backing operation it does not cut into the first and last pages of the text. The amount of hotmelt applied should always be as small as it is safe to use.

Pumped and pressurized units

When pump- or pressure-type applicators are used, endeavour to find a hotmelt that is of low-viscosity, as this will require only very low air pressures to move the adhesive around.

Combined endsheets

Endpapers with step-up ribbons have been covered earlier (p. 42).

Gluing-off or first gluing

The object of this operation is to seal the sewn sections together to form a firm yet roundable book block. The adhesive chosen should have:

1 Low-viscosity with high solids content, in order to flow in between the signatures but not up the sewing holes.

2 The ability to hold a round.

---

* The cockling or introduction of waves into the first and last pages is not always due to the endpaper adhesives; it can also be attributed to the grain direction, or to the use of too much heat during the printing process, especially if the endpapering operation is performed within a short period of time.

With emulsions, stretching of the paper will be observed by the waves or cockle; with hotmelts, the bond will be so strong that when the paper eventually takes up some moisture again the wave or cockle will be seen.

3 Compatibility with the lining adhesive (check the type of adhesive to be used). It is not possible to use an emulsion for gluing-off and then to apply a hotmelt for lining without having a paper membrane between, or very specially adapted machinery.

4 The ability to be easily cleaned from the spine brushes.

5 The inability for the books to block together when stacked.

Problem area

The main cause of problems is the application of too much adhesive (Figure 8.1). This means either that the film thickness and tenacity are stronger than the coating on some papers, or that no round can be achieved. This can first be observed when the book paper is seen to split.

Figure 8.1 Gluing-off or first-gluing guide

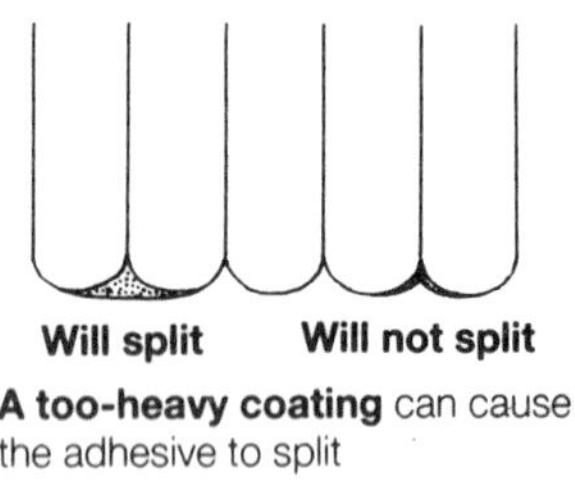

A too-heavy coating can cause the adhesive to split

The emulsion should form a thin skin over the folds or bolts of the signatures, not a solid wedge of adhesive from one signature to the next. The gluing-off emulsion chosen should be tested, taking into consideration the next operation; for flat-back work a firmer spine may be desired, but if the operation of rounding and backing is to follow then due consideration should be given to the adhesive's forming capabilities.

Caution Gluing-off emulsion will flow up the sew holes extensively if the paper is hard and no subsequent smashing has taken place to close the punch and needle holes.

Single lining with emulsion

The lining of book blocks is normally performed using emulsion adhesives; the product should be chosen after consideration of the following:

1 type of applicator;

2 drying process;

3 subsequent bindery operation.

Book blocks that have subsequently to be rounded should have a flexible but firm emulsion and a stretchable lining material. If on one machine the adhesive has to be first pumped up to a feeder tank and then flow down an application tube, it must be pump-stable and have an acceptable flow. If a product is not pump-stable and breaks down then the flow could be too great and the adhesive would flow too far between the signatures and certainly into any sew holes. Conversely, if it thickens then this will cause adhesive starvation. Lining machines with roller applicators, applying the emulsion to the spine of the book and to the liner, require a high tack adhesive to hold the lining material in place during the cutting operation and resist spine swell. When RF/HF-assisted drying is used the choice of emulsion is critical because the vibration of the molecules creates so much heat that the emulsion must be designed to resist a drop in tack levels as the emulsion heats up; it must also have the ability to hold against the tendency to swell, otherwise an unsatisfactory spine will be observed.

A temperature of 60–70 °C is often registered as a book emerges from the RF–HF tunnel. This has to be reduced to 23–25 °C before the book enters the three-knife trimmers.

Hotmelt single lining

Hotmelt single lining is proving to be very successful, especially if large punch and needle holes cannot be sealed before the lining operation. It also offers a greater amount of insurance if coated or heavily inked areas are observed on the signature folds. The lining material should have a good stretchability and it is generally agreed that a hotmelt that is preheated before rounding holds the shape better as it chills in the moulded form. The over-application of hotmelt is not recommended as this makes the gaining of a good round difficult.

Roundable hotmelts with a good stretch and very low shrink-back (see Chapter 5, p. 43 on unsewn book blocks to be rounded and backed) are now being used in this operation when no preheater has been fitted to the rounder and backer.

Care must be taken when setting the liner nip station as insufficient spine pressure will result in bubbles appearing after the trimming operation.

Double-or triple-lining units

Two basic types exist, as follows:

1 The book block is held between belts with the spine facing downwards. The book moves over a shaped glue roller, which is a part of an animal-glue tank. The roller can be changed or turned so that its shape will match the spine round. A shaped scraper is used to control the coating weight. The first adhesive application of a firm but flexible animal glue of between 60 and 70 per cent solids is applied. The product must have sufficient tack to hold the mull or hinge material until it reaches the second adhesive applicator, which applies a further film of adhesive.

This adhesive has normally been slightly diluted to reduce the tack level, so resisting any pulling of the mull material. A brown crêpe or kraft paper is used to hold in the shape of the book. The book block then moves over a damp roller which presses the mull-adhesive-crêpe sandwich firmly together.

2 On the second type of lining unit, the adhesive is fed via a shaped applicator that forms a part of the adhesive tank. A shaped silicone-rubber roller transfers the adhesive down on to the upward-facing book spine. The mull is then placed on top, and a further application of adhesive accepts the kraft liner. The main criteria for selecting the adhesive for these machines are good tack and no stringing, in order to produce a firm, dry film to hold in the shape. Special emulsion adhesives have been produced to replace the traditional animal glues for this operation, not only to give consistent viscosity and quality but an increase in the life expectancy of the book, especially in the central heated home.

Headbanding

Head- and tailbands are attached to the lining paper using an emulsion that gives good adhesion to synthetic or cotton materials. The applicators are normally gravity-fed nozzle applicators, and, providing the adhesive has got a high grab and is fast setting, the viscosity range can be 2–6000 centipoises (cP). The adhesive must not affect the polythene tubing and should preferably be easy-clean so that piping can be washed out quickly and efficiently.

Casing-in

The machines that perform this operation are divided as regards adhesive application between older paste-pot types, semi-automatics and the newer pump or recirculating adhesive applicator systems.

For casing-in generally, the adhesive must give a good, non-blistering bond on to the case board as well as on to the lap of the surface material. It must have the ability to move or flow through the mull or binge material. The adhesive must not affect or be affected by PVC materials and tests should be carried out to ensure that the adhesive and materials are compatible.

Older and semi-automatic casing-in machines require a pasty, high-viscosity adhesive with an element of thixotropy: a viscosity of 10 000–18 000 cP and a solids content of 28–61 per cent are frequently used. Major elements of the adhesive must be its flow and sheer down for application, but it must also not be able to leak or drip, as it is liable to from some of the older paste-pot units. The adhesive should not skin, and with the aid of a damp cloth or plastic film should stay open from one day's production to the next.

Automatic pump-and-return casing-in machines operate by pumping adhesives in the viscosity range of 1500-3500 cPs up into the crutch of the applicator and governing rollers. The excess adhesive is returned by a flow pipe. It is advisable to restrict the flow so that the returned pipe does not get overfilled, and also not to pump adhesive round while it is not being used, as it will only lose moisture to the atmosphere. The adhesive should be tested for pump stability as well as its ability to bond all the materials required of it. It should also not bond fully until it has entered the building-in unit, when, after the pressing, it should give fibre tear.

Special high-speed casing-in machines are now available in which the application of the adhesive is via a stencil or matrix, which then glues out the case. The adhesive has to have a good tack, but must not skin or thicken in the glue tank. An in-line, high-speed machine is capable of casing-in flat-back books at 240 cases per minute, and as the books are generally for children the adhesive must bond on to plastic laminate material. Make sure you are using the correct adhesive that will give a commercially acceptable bond. Inspect copy samples that are at least three months old, read the adhesive data sheet, or ask your adhesive supplier to do tests for you.

Joint gluing

The correct joint glue should bond or give fibre tear after the book has passed the building-in unit. It must not leach under pressure and heat. The correct choice of a hotmelt joint glue will help reduce the joint heat and even make it possible to build-in the joints cold. Hotmelts used should be special ones or else must be chosen with care as some of them can stain.

The adhesive must be correctly applied right into the shoulder of the book, otherwise the book block will drop out of its case (Figure 8.2).

Figure 8.2
Joint gluing

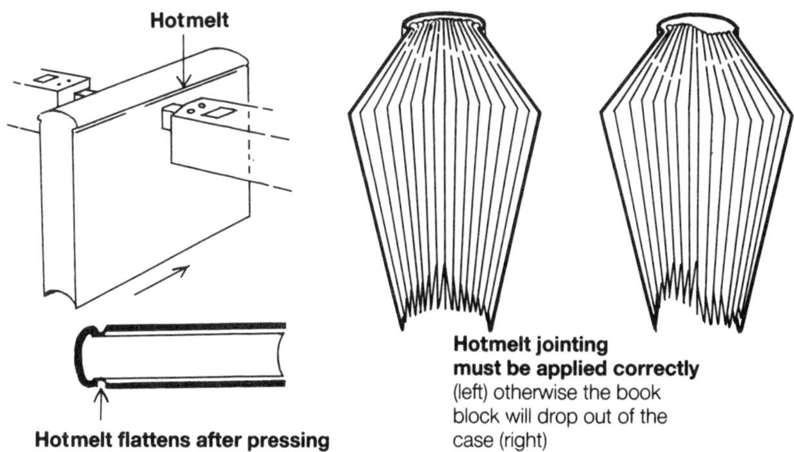

Case making

The art of case making is to produce an attractive book-block protector that stays flat and resists warp.

The case maker should produce consistently, whatever the ambient temperature or humidity.

Low-cost animal adhesives are normally affected by temperature. They can lose their tack, which allows the turnover to move and generally causes problems by not being warp-resistant. Higher-quality animal adhesives do not have unpleasant odours owing to the higher standard of raw materials used.

Adhesives with a viscosity of about 300 cP at 155 °C, which are used at 55-65 °C and have a high gell power with no stringing, are normally preferred for conventional case-making machinery.

High-speed case-making machines are now being produced to run in excess of 120 cases per minute. It is generally agreed that these require a different grade of animal glue than, say, the rotary case maker which requires a lower-viscosity, longer open-time product.

The adhesives should not be over-diluted and the following guidelines should be noted:

1 Never add oils or fats, as these will leach out over the coming months.

2 Keep dirty buckets and cloths out of the bindery, as these will encourage mould spores.

9 Glossary of bookbinding terms

Adhesive binding Unsewn binding; same as perfect bound and patent bound; pages of book bound with adhesive.

Back The part of the book nearest the fold.

Back lining The bookbinding operation involving the back of a book, which has been previously sewn or glued, whereby the backs of the sections are spread outwards from the centre of the book. This adds to the permanence of the 'rounding' and provides an abutment for the cover boards.

Backup disc A brass disc holding the bottom back edge of the book block while the rougher roughs the backbone.

Blocking (1) The impression of letters, normally in gold.

Blocking (2) When books stick together owing to tacky adhesive film.

Boards The chipboards forming the internal structure of case; *see* Casebound.

Body (1) The main part of a book.

Body (2) Thickness of book, type of paper, etc.

Bolt The folded edge of the sheet before cutting.

Building-in machine A machine used for the rapid drying of cased books. By means of several applications of heat and pressure, books are dried in a matter of seconds. This is an alternative to lengthy pressure in a 'standing press'.

Bulk Same as Body (2); some papers give more bulk.

Burst Slit or perforate the signature prior to folding.

Burst-bound Adhesive-bound, using a burst or perforate backbone, in contrast to cut-off perfect bound.

Cameron line Printing line, from roll stock and feeding signatures to book block, direct to adhesive binding line.

Camming Interrupting application of adhesive by camming (lifting) the doctor blade closed on the glue wheel.

Case (1) A cover consisting of two boards, a hollow, and a cover material.

Case (2) The stiff cover of a book.

Casebound Fully bound, as distinct from paper-covered; same as hardbound and edition bound.

Case making Forming the case by gluing the boards to the cover material.

Casing-in Inserting the book block into the case.

Casing-in paste An adhesive used in bonding the book block to the case.

Centre spread A centre opening where the print travels across two pages.

Coated paper A general term for paper on the surface of which a mineral (e.g. clay) is applied after the body paper has been made.

Collate Bring together the sections of a book, i.e. gather and collate.

Coloured edges Edges tinted with a brushed-on agent. The adhesive must not inhibit staining.

Combined endsheets Endsheets bonded to a centre strip. These become the cover of an adhesive-bound book prior to casing-in.

Contents The page that lists articles and chapters.

Cover The paper, board, cloth and/or leather (used singly or combined) to which the body of a book is secured. The cover of an edition-bound book is called a 'case'.

Cover drum A metal wheel that positions the cover on to the backbone of a book.

Covering Positioning and gluing a cover on a side-stitched magazine or book.

Crash A loose-woven cloth, or mesh, used to reinforce the book block in the case.

Cut-backed Having had the bolts cut off by the binding machine and backed with glue.

Cut edges All three edges cut by guillotine.

Drawn-on cover A soft cover glued to a sewn or wire-stitched book block.

Dummy A plain-paper test copy.

Edges The cut edges of a book.

Edition or hard-case binding Gluing book into a hard cover, as with textbooks, dictionaries, and encyclopedias.

Endpaper The first and last leaves of book; last leaf used for casing-in.

Endsheets The leaves of paper glued to the outside signatures. The outside endsheets are glued to the book case (casing-in).

Even pages Those pages numbered with even numbers.

First gluing The gluing immediately after sewing.

Flush Term describing the limp cover of a book cut flush with the paper.

Fly A sheet folded once to produce four pages, i.e. endpapers.

Folio to foot A page number at the foot of a page.

Foot The bottom of the book.

Foredge The front of the book; the margin on the outside edge.

Forward Lining a book between binding or sewing and casing-in.

Gathering The process of assembling in their proper order the folded sections of a book. This can be done by hand or on a large mechanical gatherer, the latter being usual in modern binderies.

Gilt edges Edges covered in a gold leaf.

Glued-back A paper cover glued to the back of a book.

Gluing-off A stage in the binding of a book after sewing, nipping and cutting, but prior to rounding and backing. The object is to cause glue to penetrate to a limited degree between the sections, thereby strengthening the effect of sewing.

Grain direction The direction in which the majority of fibres lie in a sheet of paper. After the pulp flows on to the moving web of a papermaking machine, the fibres tend to lie parallel with one another in the direction of the movement. On being wetted with adhesives, paper swells to a greater degree across the grain than in the grain direction, and it is of importance in bookbinding for this and other reasons that the paper used for the text should be made so that the grain direction runs from head to tail in the finished book. The terms 'grain direction' and 'machine direction' are synonymous.

Ground wood A paper pulp made by mechanically grinding wood, as distinct from pulp made by cooking or digesting wood chips in a solution of soda or other chemicals. Ground-wood paper is of low grade.

Gutter An imposition term: internal gap between facing pages.

Half-bound A casebound book with stronger back and corners.

Head The top of the book.

Headband A narrow band of decorative fabric. Headbands are glued to the head and tail of the book backbone, or sometimes only to the head.

Hinge The joint of a flexible-covered book; *see* Joint.

Hollow A strip of board in the centre of a case to stiffen the spine.

Imperfection A book incorrectly bound.

Imposition Arranging the pages of a book for printing; this determines how folding is done.

Insert A glued-in section.

Jacket Paper dust-cover over the case.

Joint (hinges) The parts on either side of a book block on which the boards hinge; the abutments formed for the case in rounding and backing.

Lay edge The edge laid against the front; on a folding machine the grip edge.

Leaf Two backing pages of a book.

Limp binding Binding with a soft cover.

Lining-up The giving of strength and firmness to the back of a book by gluing a strip of crash or scrim to it after adhesive binding or sewing and nipping. The crash or scrim should extend to ¼ inch from the head and tail of the book and project 1¼ inches on either side for fixing to the endsheets; this is known as 'first lining'. It is then covered with a strip of paper the full size of the back; this is 'second lining'.

Margin The white space around the type area.

McCain sewing A method of sewing a book–through the sides instead of the backbone.

Nipping Pressing book blocks after sewing to remove bulk and air.

Nipping station Where unsewn books have their spines pressed in.

Offside Part of the case at the edge of the book as opposed to the front.

One-shot hotmelt Common name for flexible, perfect-binding, hotmelt-type products.

One-up One book per clamp, as in magazine binding. *See* Two-up.

Padding Edges adhesively bound for easy peel-out.

Page One side of a leaf.

Pagination The page numbers of a book.

Patent binding Unsewn binding.

Perforated binding Adhesive binding, where signature folds are not cut off but perforated.

Perforation Holes punched to let out air or let in glue.

Press pasting Adhesive bonding of signature sheets to each other on the press. Also called internal tipping.

Quadfolder front The front edges of a book not trimmed but left rough; signature folded on a quadfolder.

Register ribbon A market bonded to the spine which comes down through the book.

Reverse roll coater An adhesive applicator with two rolls and no spinner; the second roll revolves against the direction of the book and thereby meters adhesive.

Roughing The preparation of a book backbone prior to adhesive application. The treatment exposes the fibre of each page to provide greater bonding area.

Rounding and backing *Rounding*: giving a book a convex appearance and a concave foredge. *Backing*: producing projecting shoulders.

Saddle stitch A method of stitching brochures or pamphlets by placing them open astride a saddle-shaped support and stitching through the back.

Sewing Fastening together the sections of a book with thread.

Sheerdown Lowering of viscosity due to the sheer from two rollers or a roller and scraper.

Shoulder A projection by rounding and backing to help hold the book in the case.

Side stitch To bind a pamphlet by wiring or sewing the sheets together sideways.

Signature A folded book-section. A book is printed on wide sheets or a web of paper, which are cut and folded into a signature. Abbreviation: sig.

Smashing Pressing a book in a machine, after sewing, to compress the pages and expel air from between them. Also known as 'nipping'.

Smyth sewing A method of sewing signatures in a book. The thread passes through the book's backbone.

Spine The centre part of the case of a book when it is cased-on.

Spinner A small, heated, rotating metal cylinder, located a few inches away from the adhesive applicator wheels on a perfect binder, which meters excess adhesive from a book being perfect bound.

Square back The back of a book block that is bound but not rounded.

Stitching Passing thread or wire through the whole contents of the book. If the book is in gathered sections then the stitching will pass from side to side about $\frac{1}{8}$ inch from the back.

Stripping A glued-off strip wrapped round a narrow-backboned book;

or a reinforced strip on the first and last signatures of a McCain-sewn book.

Tail The bottom edge of a book.

Tight back A book cover glued to the body of the book at the back.

Tipping on, tipping in Gluing a separate sheet on or in.

Trimmed edge An edge that has been cut and left ragged and irregular.

Two-up Binding in units of two which are subsequently cut in the middle making two books, as with the *Reader's Digest*, *TV Guide*, and paperbacks.

Uncut foredges The result of bad trimming of a book, leaving it with some bolts not cut.

Unsewn book Cut-backed book bound with wire or adhesive.

Unsewn lining Cut-backed books glued and lined.

Wire stabbing A method of binding magazines with staples.

Wrapped round Illustrations printed in sets of four pages, with the text inserted in the middle.

Yapp The edges of the cover material which overlaps the cut edge of the book block, as e.g. in a soft bible.